MANY PATHS, ONE PURPOSE

Career Paths for Social Work and Human Services Majors

Edited by

Tuyen D. Nguyen

D0451345

University Press of America,® Inc.
Lanham · Boulder · New York · Toronto · Oxford

Copyright © 2006 by
University Press of America,® Inc.
4501 Forbes Boulevard
Suite 200
Lanham, Maryland 20706
UPA Acquisitions Department (301) 459-3366

PO Box 317
Oxford
OX2 9RU, UK

Library of Congress Control Number: 2006924500
ISBN-13: 978-0-7618-3515-8 (paperback : alk. paper)
ISBN-10: 0-7618-3515-6 (paperback : alk. paper)

CONTENTS

INTRODUCTION

This book is written specifically for those who have made a decision to work in the human services and social work profession, but are not clear in which career track to pursue. A professional has contributed each chapter in this book with personal experiences working in a particular career track of the human services field. Therefore, the reader should get an insider's view of what it is like to be working in a certain career track. The main intent of the book is to provide an overview of each human services field so that the reader will be better informed of the various career paths which one can take, based on a variety of critical elements specified in each chapter. There are fifteen chapters in this book, covering fifteen career tracks that are outlined by the following subheadings:

Nature of the Work
Training and Degree(s) Required
Personality Traits and Skills Deemed Important to Succeed
Difficulties of the Work
Rewards of the Work
How to Get Started on This Career Track

Nature of the Work

The purpose of this section is for the reader to have an overview of the nature of the work involved and to gain perspectives regarding work conditions from an expert already in the field. This is an important part of the chapter because it gives the reader an understanding of what it is like to be in a particular social work/human services career path. Therefore, the emphasis of this section of the chapter is on helping the reader obtain an understanding of a particular career path, with respect to the nature of the work.

Training and Degree(s) Required

In this section, the author of the chapter specifies what type of education and degree(s) one needs to have and any special training that has to be completed before one can work in a particular career track. The author also includes any necessary continuing education that one may have to acquire on a yearly basis, as required by law and state boards, in order to continue working in the field.

Personality Traits and Skills Deemed Important to Succeed

In this section, each author elaborates on the known personality traits and skills that have been found among successful people in a particular social work career track. For example, in working with geriatric clients, an important personality trait deemed important is deep caring for the elderly. The author's main purpose in this section is to help the reader make an assessment of oneself to see if there is a match between one's own inherent personality traits and a particular career path under consideration.

Difficulties of the Work

In this section, the author pinpoints major difficulties of their work that professionals in the field encounter on a regular basis. The author's purpose is to help the reader look at the work realistically by reporting various difficulties which practitioners in the field struggle with. Through reading this part of the chapter the reader will have a clearer idea of what issues/difficulties that he or she will have to wrestle with once entering into the field.

Rewards of the Work

In this section, the author of the chapter concretely lays out what he or she considers to be the rewards that the work offers. The author will also take into consideration rewards other practitioners in the field have found. The author's main objective is to provide the reader with predominant rewards that keep human services professionals motivated and passionate about their work.

How To Get Started On This
Career Track

Throughout this last section, the author advises ways an individual can get on track for a particular career path in social work and human services. The author lays out directions for the reader to take with the aim of achieving his or her career track goal. The author then concludes the chapter by focusing on what the reader can do immediately. For example, taking certain college courses to put him or her on the right path to a career in social work and human services.

1

CLINICAL SOCIAL WORK IN AN **AIDS** SERVICE ORGANIZATION

ೞೲ

Monica A. Carbajal, LMSW
Derek Robertson, M. Ed., LPC
Shawna Stewart, MA, LPC

This chapter highlights the perils and rewards of social work within the HIV/AIDS population utilizing the experiences from the clinical staff at the AIDS Outreach Center (AOC). AOC, a leading organization located in Fort Worth Texas serves men, women and children with HIV and their families. Its mission is to serve those with HIV while educating the public about HIV prevention and advocating for sound HIV public policy. Licensed master level social workers and licensed professional counselors make up the clinical department. In 2003, the clinical department provided mental health services to over 350 clients a near 40 percent increase from the previous year 2003[1] (AIDS Outreach Center Annual Report 2003). Their experiences and knowledge are documented in hopes of offering encouragement and sparking interest in this much needed area where the skills of clinical social work can be utilized within the client base of people living with HIV/AIDS.

An AIDS Service Organization (ASO) can be a challenging and exciting place for a social work clinician to work. Twenty plus years into the pandemic, clients still face a lot of stigma. The stigma has lessened, but clients must deal with a level of discrimination in areas such as housing, employment and occasionally from medical personnel. Most people are aware that there are treatments for HIV/AIDS. Many young people have never known a world without AIDS. As a result, complacency or fatigue has set in and HIV/AIDS no longer gets the attention it once did. Sadly, this has resulted in increasing infection rates in almost all categories- even with gay men who were once the model of how behavior can change through education.

Nature of the Work

When working at an HIV/AIDS service organization, a social worker's caseload will be very diverse. Once thought of as a disease limited to gay men and IV drug users, AIDS today is seen in all populations, age groups, gender groups and socio-economic strata. The National Center for HIV, STD and TB prevention ([1]2003) noted despite prevention efforts an estimated 40,000 Americans continue to become infected with HIV each year. The racial make up of the HIV pandemic continues to be primarily Caucasian, but one half of new infections in men and 2/3 of new infections in women are in the African American community[2] (Center for Disease Control 2004). Dealing with HIV infection in African-American men who have sex with men presents a challenge. Blackwell[3] (2000) notes the issue of being gay and an African-American from a cultural standpoint exerts inexplicable fear of disclosing, not ones HIV status, but the greatest fear is disclosing one's sexual preference. This fear causes continued spread of the virus from lack of notifying previous partners and /or fearing a demand to explain the source of their own infection. Likewise in the Latino community a study spanning between 1999-2002, showed the rate of reported HIV diagnosis were up 26 percent overall[4] (National Center for HIV, STD & TB Prevention, 2003).

Non-white ethnic groups are being hard hit by the disease and many in these groups fall below poverty level. Services to address basic needs, and that are culturally aware are imperative for an HIV/AIDS social worker. Cultural awareness and knowledge are also needed in regard to the gay community, which continues to be hard hit by the disease. A social worker must be able to put aside her own moral/religious issues and be ready to show unconditional positive regard toward her clients. Because of the stigma HIV/AIDS still has in society, and the discrimination clients with HIV/AIDS get from their own individual sub-groups, many people are fearful of going to an agency for help stemming from their HIV status. Mindfulness of this fear and acceptance on all levels will make clients more likely to obtain services and get the help they need. At times, client/clinician boundaries are more malleable than in other settings. It is not unusual for social workers in an ASO to do home visits, seek out clients who have missed sessions, visit them in the hospital or when they are sick and/or dying. Because some clients get only minimal physical contact, due to ignorance about HIV transmission modes, hugging clients at the end of a session is quite common. Work in supervision with respect to transference and counter-transference helps clinicians to be mindful of when the client/counselor boundaries have become too pliable.

The disenfranchised of our society are seen in HIV/AIDS agencies: homosexuals, minority populations, the impoverished, homeless, mentally ill, addicts, criminals, and prostitutes. Many of these people lack the basic necessities of life and will need help in finding and accessing local resources to help meet these basic needs. Social workers will need to remember Maslow's Hierarchy of Needs when helping their HIV/AIDS clients. Clients who do not know where they will sleep that night or who are struggling with physical illness will not make discussing emotional issues a priority. It is very important to use sessions to work with clients on issues that are most relevant to them at the moment.

When ASO's opened in the 1980's and 1990's, one of their main focuses was helping clients prepare to die. Since 1996, when the AIDS medication "cocktails" were prescribed, people with HIV and AIDS have been living longer. The focus is no longer on death preparation but on addressing how to live with HIV or AIDS. The number of people seen in agencies has increased, as has the length of time they receive services. In the last five years, funding has remained steady for agencies, but the infection rate has steadily increased. Social workers find themselves having to provide services for more people without an increase in funding. Because clients are dying at a decreased rate, social workers are counseling their clients on many other issues besides death. Depression, relationship problems, work and money problems are common themes. Many clients have experienced childhood or adult sexual abuse as well. There are also a disproportionate number of clients who suffer from chronic mental illness, especially major depression, bipolar disorder, schizophrenia, and borderline personality disorder. Clients with borderline IQ's are also seen at an increasingly high rate. These clients, because of their lack of skills and knowledge, and because of their vulnerability in being victimized are taken advantage of are at high risk of HIV infection. Social workers need a working knowledge of safer sex techniques and must be comfortable in discussing specific sexual issues. Because the stress in funding is toward prevention, it is important to reach those who are at risk for infection, and to address at risk behaviors, which are sex and IV drug use. America tends to be conservative about discussing matters related to sex. But if the clinician is not comfortable talking with clients about sex and at risk behaviors, she/he can project feelings of shame and guilt upon their clients and thus reduce the likelihood of the client returning for much needed services. Education, conversations and research about sexual issues that are unfamiliar to the clinician will prepare her for client sessions and reduce the "shock value" of what may be heard.

The Importance of Community Groups

The stigma of HIV still resonates throughout many communities. AOC attempts to combat this by offering cohesive groups. Believing in the importance of offering cohesive groups, AOC provides opportunity for individuals to gather and discuss the challenges of living with HIV/AIDS with others in their same gender, ethnicity, sexual orientation, age and/or specific area of concern. Experience with newly diagnosed clients has taught counselors at AOC that those clients who meet others who have been living with the disease come to accept their situation much more quickly and are more likely to follow through with treatment.

Therapeutic groups are led by an AOC counselor to lend a more therapeutic, process tone while other formed groups that offer more of a social outlet are led by staff members working with that particular population. A social outlet for clients can be as important as a therapeutic one as many clients live with HIV/AIDS in secret for fear of rejection. When attending a group, the person feels included and accepted fully. The following is a list of current groups offered at AOC for HIV positive clients unless otherwise noted: Gay Men's Support Group, Sisita to Sista Group for women, Latino Group for Spanish-speaking men and women, Positive Living Support Group for men and women, Positive Recovery Substance Abuse Group for men and women , Auricular Acupuncture for men and women in recovery, Teen Time for children ages 13-18 infected or affected by HIV/AIDS, Teen Support Group for HIV positive teens and Therapy Group for gay male survivors of sex abuse.

The clinical social worker can lend their therapeutic expertise by developing and presenting topic material based on the needs of the agency's clients. Two such examples are the recent addition of a support group for HIV positive teens and a therapy group for gay male survivors of sex abuse. Observing the increase of positive teens not only coming to AOC for services, but the realization that former HIV positive children were now in their mid teens, the need was responded to by adding a separate group to address their special needs and issues. Likewise, when clinicians took note that a high percentage of current and previous male clients had a history of sexual abuse, the response was to offer a therapeutic group to address the need.

The clinical social worker in an ASO should be mindful of client needs, similarities, areas where services are lacking or are inadequate and advocate to meet the needs of their clients at every age level.

Training, Degree, License Required

For the professional social worker, the Master's degree in social work is the preferred degree in addition, the Advanced Clinical licensure is a requirement in most counseling settings for the purpose of billing for services to Medicare or other form of insurance. Opportunities to participate in educational workshops or seminars relating to HIV/AIDS populations are encouraged. Every state has some form of state HIV/AIDS conference where new information is presented. Due to the discriminatory vulnerability of clients in the area of HIV/AIDS, advocacy is a highly utilized skill. Advocacy and teaching clients to advocate for themselves, is a lesson that can be carried over in every area of their life.

Personality Traits, Skills Deemed
Important to Succeed

Due to the wide range of clientele seen in ASO's it is vital that the clinical social worker be knowledgeable of various mental health issues including diagnosis and familiarity with the Diagnostic and Statistical Manual of Mental Disorders, the DSM. The counseling staff have at times been the first point of entry for clients wishing to address issues stemming from their HIV/AIDS diagnosis only to realize a chronic mental disorder was not previously diagnosed. A strong knowledge base of community resources adds to the effectiveness of the clinical social worker in the HIV/AIDS service arena. At times the social worker must take an active role in educating their client on a particular service and how one can obtain and benefit from a particular agency or program. For example, the clinical social worker may take time to explain how to access social security benefits, state medication programs, county medication programs, county medical and mental health programs and area resources for basic needs such as clothing, furniture and child care. Although outside the traditional realm of clinical services, these are just a few examples of resources the clinical social worker can help teach clients in an ASO to access. Again, meeting the basic needs of the client can then allow the client to properly focus on their clinical issues thus meeting the need of the whole person and enhancing the chances of a sustained positive change.

As social workers the code of ethics calls us to serve clients without regard to personal differences or belief systems. This principle is especially important in this service arena. Arguably, the arena of ASO's is one that the call to service is practiced to the highest degree. The clinical social worker must be prepared to work with a diverse clientele. An openness and willingness to understand different cultural, ethnic and economic backgrounds are highly sought traits that will lead to success. It is important to take note of traits that can cause fatigue and 'burn out' in this type of clinical setting. Personalizing hostility, personal judgements and poor boundaries can lead to frustrations. As previously mentioned, for many clients, HIV infections is just one of many factors in their lives. The clinician can become a safe target for these frustrations to play out and therefore, the clinician must be willing to take note of this and address the matter with the client in therapeutic method. In addition, self-determination of the client must be accepted. The client base of the clinical social worker may include clients who for example, have refused medical care for their HIV infection, or who have decided to quit medical care and exercise their right to quality rather than quantity of life. A judgmental clinician may inadvertently aggravate the situation. Mistrust and shame can be the result, significantly hindering a clinician's ability to continue assisting the client.

Many clients are very grateful for the services they receive. For many, clinical services in an ASO are the only clinical services ever received. However, one tends to remember the clients who were not appreciative. Healthy boundaries and organizational support including clinical supervision with a clinical supervisor or colleague is of vital importance to acquire longevity in an ASO.

Difficulties of the Work

Case Story: *Pablo is a 34 year- old Guatemalan male living on the street. When he sees outreach workers passing out coffee and sandwiches he approaches to receive what will be his breakfast for the day. The outreach workers explain they are also able to do testing for HIV and begin to discuss the disease, modes of transmission etc. in an effort to convince Pablo to get tested. Pablo agrees and two weeks later Pablo returns for free coffee, a sandwich and his results. He's positive. Now, the outreach workers face several dilemmas. Pablo is in the United States illegally; he cannot live in a shelter because the local shelters now require an identification card of some sort for entry. He cannot apply for any housing program for people living with HIV/AIDS because the majority of federal funding does not allow persons living illegally in the United States to have access to these programs. The outreach staff assists Pablo in securing an appointment with the local health department and are able to offer him food pantry services. Pablo has no family in the United States since the death of his wife and returning to Guatemala will leave him with no hope of securing any assistance. Pablo believes the hope of finding work and receiving basic needs such as food and clothes from homeless assistance programs are better than returning to his homeland where this would be considered a luxury. For Pablo, the hope is enough to risk staying in the United States. Pablo attends a few appointments and is seen at the pantry on occasion, but then is not heard from in several months. Pablo by chance is seen waiting on a popular street corner where other homeless men gather to hire themselves out as day laborers. The outreach staff stop and ask Pablo for an update. Pablo explains making the appointments for the doctor is difficult because he accepts jobs whenever he can. In addition, some of his HIV medications require him to eat first, something he cannot always do and therefore has suffered nausea and other side effects. Pablo tells the staff he appreciates what they have tried to do, but he has no home and securing work and saving what little money he has is the only way he'll someday meet his goal of renting a room to live in. HIV is only one of his problems.*

The case of 'Pablo' is an example of areas of frustration experienced in an ASO. The complex needs of clients are magnified when elements beyond their HIV status must be addressed first.

As the issue of HIV/AIDS continues to receive less attention and complacency continues to be demonstrated through a upward shift in infection rates, insufficient resources and funding are just two of the areas the clinical social worker will find difficult to overcome in an ASO. Funding levels are not keeping up with the infection rate. Barriers such as the above case describes are becoming more common. For these reasons the social worker has an obligation to advocate and educate both in the local community when a client confronts discrimination and at the state and federal level where decisions about funding are made.

The social worker in an ASO must be prepared for the obvious in working with the HIV/AIDS population. Stigma and discrimination exists for clients. At times, clients do suffer from side effects of their medication that make it difficult to concentrate on services provided. Finally, deaths still occur and can be trying for even the most seasoned clinician.

It is very important to have a working knowledge involving issues of discrimination, guilt, shame, side effects of medications and especially death and dying. Because of the stigma of HIV/AIDS, some clients will only have their social worker to help them with these issues. At times, the social worker may find herself as the only person at her client's deathbed. Personal feelings about death must be addressed in order to truly 'be there' for a client who is dying. The clinical social worker in the arena of HIV/AIDS, should first self analyze personal beliefs prior to accepting work in an area so filled with challenges. On many occasions, the nature of the work calls the clinical social worker to step outside the realm of a traditional clinical setting.

Rewards of the Work

Variety is the key ingredient in terms of reward in working in an ASO. The clinical social worker is able to work with a client base from every age range, ethnic background, religious background and socioeconomic level. It is an arena to learn the craft of clinical work and an opportunity to address, confront and erase any pre judgements the clinician may possess.

It is an opportunity to truly assist in healing, redefining and restoring hope in someone's life.

Case story: *"I felt unlovable, untouchable and already dead inside" said Andy a 33 year old male during one of his final counseling sessions, "but* *today I feel like I'm barely learning what it means to live- thanks for putting up with me, I'm gonna be alright."*

Because HIV/AIDS clients are so susceptible to rare and unusual diseases and medical conditions, helping clients find more information can alleviate frustration, grief and unnecessary fear. Consider the case of 'Joseph' where a lack of knowledge led to suicidal ideations. By taking time and using education as a strategy, the clinician was able to self-educate and educate the client. Suicidal thoughts were combated and overcome with knowledge.

Case story: *Joseph, a 43 year old gay male had been hospitalized numerous times within the past year. He is fearful that he will die soon. Joseph finds out he is 'leaking spinal fluid' and cannot get in to see his doctor until lab results are completed. Joseph is fearful, desperate and considers ending his life. He comes to his scheduled weekly appointment with his counselor and informs her of these new developments. Lacking knowledge of the aliment, she suggests they get online and gather informa-tion together about this condition. After looking at several medical web pages they discover it is not as rare a condition as thought. Further research leads to finding that the body replaces spinal fluid several times a day. The client reports feeling a great sense of relief and a renewed sense of hope about his condition, this sustains him until he is able to see his doctor for more information.*

How to Get Started on this
Career Track

For the aspiring social worker desiring to work in the area of HIV/ AIDS, it is important first to gain an educated understanding of the disease itself. Most local ASO offer HIV/AIDS education and provide opportunities for volunteer placement. It is highly recommended for all social workers to gain insight and knowledge in this area. Volunteering in an ASO or completing an internship in one can give a social work student an opportu-nity to experience the client base, services provided and perhaps an area they would ultimately enjoy working in. As those with HIV/AIDS continue to live longer and new infections continue to rise, schools of social work have responded with offering courses in social work and the HIV/AIDS population. Courses such as these can give a social work student a basic knowledge base in various areas in the field they may wish to pursue. Courses in counseling theories, diagnosing, therapy techniques and diversity awareness can further prepare a social worker for a career in an HIV/AIDS service organization.

Notes

1.　AIDS Outreach Center Annual Report 2003

2.　www.natap.org/2003/nov/113003_2.htm New Study shows overall increase in HIV diagnosis: African Americans, Latinos, Gay and Bisexual Men most affected. Retrieved on May 21, 2004

3.　www.cdc.gov/hiv/pub/facts/afam.htm Fact Sheet HIV/AIDS Among African Americans. Retrieved on May 21, 2004

4.　AIDS & African Americans: A guide for substance abuse, sexuality can care. Dr. Pamela Blackwell Johnson, LPC. NCD Publishing Dallas TX. 2000.

2

L' INVITATION AU VOYAGE: CAREER COUNSELING AS A PROFESSION

ℬℭ

Adam R. Malson

Nature of the Work

Many students in social work or human services approach an introductory course in career counseling or career development with apathy and loathing; many sign up for the course to simply fulfill a degree requirement. This chapter is designed to introduce you to the fields of career counseling and career development as you continue to gather career information and consider the options of your own career path. This chapter will provide you with a basic outline of the fields of career counseling and career development and will serve to give you an introductory view of the work of these two rapidly expanding fields. It is hoped that you will use this chapter as a beginning resource as you explore the realms of career counseling and career development and that you will consider these introductory ideas in the context of your work with clients.

At the onset of this chapter, it is important to draw a distinction between the fields of career counseling and career development. *Career counseling* may be described as a face-to-face therapeutic process between career counselor and client(s) that focuses primarily on the client's career-related issues (e.g. career choice, coping with job-related stress, coping with career transition, job searching, etc.) The field of *career development* attempts to explain vocational behavior, such as initial career choice, work adjustment, life-span career progress, or the sociological, economic, psychological and/or physiological forces that influence one's entry into the workforce. As researchers and theorists continue to make valuable contributions to each of these vast fields, it is important to draw as distinction between the two.

As with any profession, it is important to note historical background to understand the context of your own work in any given field. Frank Parsons, founder of the Boston vocational education movement, is considered by many to be one of the principal founders of career counseling. Parsons, well-known in his own generation as a fierce advocate for workers rights and known as an opponent of child labor, created the Vocations Bureau in 1908 in an urban neighborhood in Boston as the first formal career counseling center in the United States. Parson's Boston vocational education movement was a social justice movement aimed to address the needs of young people and displaced workers (see Parsons, 1909). This first program guided job seekers in examining their skills and interests and helped them to connect with local employment opportunities.

The fields of career counseling and career development have since greatly expanded from these early roots. Popular career development theorists such as Linda Gottfredson, John Holland, John Krumboltz, David and Anna Miller-Tiedeman, and Donald Super and have since helped to formalize the field to include broad theories on career development, client assessment in career counseling, and career development resources ranging from basic career information to individualized client career planning strategies.

Some of the most progressive modern work in the fields of career counseling and career development, however, may be found in the work of David L. Blustein, counseling psychologist who conducts research and teaches at Boston College in Chestnut Hill, MA. Drawing on the historical context of the fields of career counseling and career development, Blustein joins Parsons in identifying these fields as social justice movements striving to serve disenfranchised, under-represented, and oppressed client popula-tions. Blustein looks beyond the process of trait-factor assessment and calls the field to integrate a "psychology of working," calling for the fields to break out of white, middle class bias that has characterized the fields of career counseling and career development in recent years (see, for example, Blustein, 2001).

Given this bit of background into the fields of career counseling and career development, what do career counselors do? Figler and Bolles (1999) suggest that the work of career counseling aims to assist clients in three main areas: (1) *Gathering of information*, where clients are able to gain valuable self-information as well as information on the options in the world of work (2) *Obtaining knowledge*, where, with the assistance of a career counselor, clients obtain and organize new career information, and (3) *Obtaining of wisdom,* where clients learn how to independently seek out career information and knowledge. It is in *gathering information, obtaining knowledge,* and *obtaining wisdom* that career counseling clients are able to make more informed career-related decisions.

Career counseling is intended for those clients who are hoping to gain career-related information, knowledge, and wisdom and may be conducted in one-on-one counseling sessions or in groups such as career support groups or career classes. Career counseling specializations are expanding to include multicultural populations (e.g. Asian Americans, African Americans, lesbian, gay, bisexual, and trangendered (LGBT) populations, people with disabilities, etc.); Pope (1995) suggests that the increasing specialization of the career counseling profession is the result of the maturation process of the profession.

Where do career counselors presently work? Career counselors today are found primarily in educational settings such as elementary and secondary schools, trade schools, colleges, and universities. Career counselors can also be found in county, state, and federal agencies as well as various NGO's (Non-governmental organizations). Figler and Bowles (1999) suggest that career counseling is becoming increasingly common in the corporate world, for "as layoffs have continued, corporations have felt a greater responsibility to help those who depart and those who remain" (p. 293). Indeed, many large corporations offer several sessions of career counseling as part of a severance packages for employees who are laid-off.

Career counseling continues to extend beyond the United States and North America. In an outline of the history of career counseling in the United States, Pope (2000) suggests that since beginning under the George H.W. Bush administration and continuing in the Clinton administration, there has been a renewal in interest in the lifelong career development of the American workforce. Career counseling has expanded as career counselors from the United States now do substantial contract internationally, including the countries of the former Soviet Union, China, Hong Kong, Malaysia, Australia, Estonia, and Poland, to name just a few (see Pope, 1999).

Training and Degrees Required

As with the fields of social work and counseling, the training and education of career counselors has become more formalized in recent years. To operate as a career counselor, a Master's degree in counseling or social work serves as the minimum requirement. Though the bulk of career counselors operate with degrees from counselor education programs, there are career counselors who graduate from social work graduate programs as well. In addition to the Master's degree in social work or counseling, professional certification and licensure in one's field is also helpful. Many states, for example, offer licensure as a Licensed Mental Health Counselor (LMHC), Licensed Professional Counselor (LPC), or Licensed Clinical Social Worker (LCSW). Certification from the National Board for Certified Counselors (NBCC) as a Nationally Certified Counselor (NCC) is helpful. Additionally, many career counselors, particularly those who work in private practice or in higher education settings, seek to earn doctoral degrees in social work, counseling, or counseling psychology (Ph.D. or Ed.D) with an emphasis in career development theory and practice.

Career counseling is not as well-defined as, for example, the fields of college mental health counseling or marriage and family therapy and there is some debate in the field over what career counseling actually is. Career counseling often gets confused with "career advising" or other forms of job-search assistance such as resume preparation or career workshops and is in many cases mischaracterized by career centers or employment agencies. As with many of the specializations outlined in this text, it is important that someone interested in exploring career counseling and career development find a good mentor and supervisor who works as at least a master's-level clinician. For a student seeking training as a career counselor, it is important to work under the supervision of a licensed and experienced career counselor during your training.

Types of Career Intervention

Career interventions vary in scope and size. Career counseling, one such intervention, is a face-to-face therapeutic process between client(s) and career counselor. Career development workshops, job shadowing programs, informational interviewing, and computer programs are other examples of career interventions. Each of these interventions are briefly outlined here.

Individual Career Counseling

Though career counseling may take place on an individual or group level, research over the past 55 years has indicated that individual career counseling is the most effective career intervention. Whiston, Sexton, & Lasoff (1998), for example, verified in a meta-analysis of the effectiveness of career interventions including workshops, computer programs, career classes, etc. that individual career counseling is the most effective intervention when measuring client change.

There are many models for conducting career counseling. Gysbers, Heppner, and Johnson (1998) offer one such representational model: 1.) an opening phase where establishment of the relationship 2.) in information gathering phase where assessment and identification of a client's "problems" or issues takes place; and 3.) A working phase where goals are set and a career action plan is made; and 4.) A final phase in which career counselor and client bring a closure to the relationship. Most experts in career counseling agree that career counseling typically involves a beginning or initial phase, a middle or working phase, and an ending or termination phase.

Career Development Workshops

Career development workshops also serve as an effective career intervention. One of the many advantages of career workshops is that career information may be disseminated to large groups of people in short amount of time. Workshops can range from being a one-time, single day workshop or be a workshop program that meets regularly over a set period of time.

The topics of career development workshops will vary widely depending on the reason for offering the workshops and the client population being served. Career workshops offered for a large group of recently laid-off factory workers might deal with explaining unemployment benefits or providing the group with the necessary tools for a job-search for experienced workers, while workshops offered to college seniors might highlight an entry-level job search or assist students in explore graduate school opportunities. In planning in implementing career development workshops, it is important to consider the client population being served.

Job Shadowing Programs and Informational Interviews

Many career counselors aid their clients in setting up job shadowing programs and in encouraging client's to pursue informational interviews. Both of these career interventions hold the similar goal of gathering information about a given career field for the client to make a more informed career decision. Professional job shadowing involves encouraging the client to spend anywhere from a few hours to several weeks observing a professional in her or his field. Job shadowing allows a client to experience first-hand the current working conditions and challenges faced by professionals in a given field. Helping clients set up a job shadowing experience is relatively easy as most working professionals welcome the idea of hosting someone who is interested in observing their daily work-life.

Informational interviewing is another useful career intervention that career counselors often suggest to their clients. Opposed to a formal job interview, a client can request an informational interview from a potential employer for the purposes of gathering information about a particular job or field. During the informational interview, one can find out about the day-to-day work of a profession, inquire about internships and job shadowing experiences, and gather further information on the job titles and job descriptions of a given field. Informational interviewing can also help clients in securing internship experiences and assist the client to establish a network of professional contacts. This network of professional contacts many times helps the client to eventually secure employment interviews.

Computer-Based Career Interventions

Computer-based career interventions have played a vital role in career development and career counseling in the past 30 years (Iaccarino, 2000). There are many computer-based career interventions available individuals as well as career counselors working with individuals. SIGI-Plus, *Discover®* program, and O*NET are among the most recognized and commonly used of these interventions; brief descriptions of each of these computer-based career interventions are offered here.

The System of Interactive Guidance (SIGI) - Plus was developed by Martin Katz at the Educational Testing Service (ETS). SIGI-Plus is primarily intended for use by college students and includes sections on self-assessment, information on possible career paths, and an outline of skills required for each career path. Additional sections offer an outline of requirements for entry into a given career, and assistance in helping users reach decisions by evaluating and combining 1.) The desirability of each occupation the client is considering; and 2.) Their chances of success in entering it. SIGI-plus, which focuses on occupations that require two or more years of college and may not be appropriate for all clients.

Another widely used computer-based career intervention is *Discover®*, developed by the American College Testing Program. Like SIGI-Plus, it is an interactive program where clients can gather extensive career information. Users complete interest and values inventories, and these in turn can be used to generate a list of related occupations. When the related occupations are listed, information on over 3,000 two-and four-year institutions that may offer course or programs of study related to occupations users have identified. These files contain data regarding cost, size, admissions policies, minority representation, male-to-female ratios, etc.

Where *Discover®* and SIGI-Plus are examples of computerized assessment systems, the US Department of Labor (DOL)'s O*NET (*Occupational Information Network*) is an example of an online career information clearinghouse. The DOL has here provided a wide range of materials that define job requirements and worker profiles, a forecast of future trends for different occupations, and a description of work environments. O*NET, which underwent significant overhaul and improvement in November, 2003, offers the most up-to-date comprehensive source of occupational information as it is continuously updated. O*NET is divided into three main sections: 1.) The *O*NET Database*; 2.) *O*NET Online*; and 3.) *O*NET Career Exploration Tools*. The DOL claims that over 95% of U.S. workers are found in this group of 1,222 occupations. A detailed description of O*NET and its three main sections may be found at http://www.doleta.gov/programs/onet (DOL, 1998).

Personality Traits and Skills Deemed Important to Succeed

In exploring the personality traits important for success as a career counselor, it is important to explore the skills necessary to perform the work of a career counselor. Figler and Bowles (1999) deemed 12 skills vitally important to the career counselor. These 12 skills are:

1. *Clarifying content*: The ability to restate the essence of the client's statement;

2. *Reflecting feeling*: Mirroring the emotional quality of the client's response, and identifying attached thoughts and feelings;

3. *Open-ended questioning*: Asking questions that explore the fullest range of possible client responses;

4. *Skill identifying*: Naming the specific areas of talent or strength revealed a client's past experience;

5. *Value clarifying*: Identifying the sources of enjoyment and satisfaction in a client's life;

6. *Creative imagining*: Methods encouraging the client to envision job and career possibilities through brain-storming, visualization, fantasizing, etc;

7. *Information giving*: Key pieces of job or career information that enable the client to understand a career-related process (such as job hunting);

8. *Role-playing*: Acting out employment-related scenarios;

9. *Spot-checking, e.g.*: "Are we going down the right track? Is this the type of work you're hoping to do?";

10. *Summarizing*: Collecting what the client has said thus far, and reviewing it or purposes of moving forward;

11. *Task setting*: Encouraging the client to engage in experiences that are directly relevant to her job or career objectives;

12. *Establishing the Yes, Buts*: Identifying the client's chief concerns, main obstacles or roadblocks s/he believes may stand in the way of her/his career goals.

What then are some personality traits of the career counselor? The career counselor is one that seeks knowledge of various social systems, e.g. economic, social, and educational systems and can articulate that knowledge to her or his clients. A career counselor is able to organize and prioritize responsibility and help clients to the same. The career counselor must possess the empathy, honesty, candor, and ability to build trust and rapport with clients. Creativity in solving problems and an intense interest in helping others find solutions to their dilemmas is important. Further, the career counselor must have a fundamental interest in the lives of his or her clients and should enjoy helping clients to realize their hopes and dreams in the context of their careers and working lives. As you have probably realized as you read the chapters of this text, many of the skills required of a career counselor are skills required of many fields in the helping professions.

It is in the context of working with clients that the importance of your counseling skills and personality traits will become apparent. Many career counselors report that one of the challenges of the work is that the personalities, skills, interests, values, abilities, and life circumstances of clients wildly vary. One session may involve work with a client who does not have the desired skill set for the career of his or her dreams, where the next session may involve a client who has the skills desired by many employers but the client reports difficulty making career decisions or making a career commitment. In career counseling, the type of client or reported client issues will vary wildly. The skills and personality traits outlined above will help a career counselor in adjusting to a diverse client population and will enable the career counselor to create individualized client intervention plans.

Difficulties of the Work

Many career counselors cite limited resources available within the organization they work for to be a major difficulty of their work. In some cases, career counselors are expected to perform the work of career counseling in addition to many other administrative tasks such as teaching, supervision, budget management, and project management. With career counseling sessions lasting anywhere from a half-hour to an hour or more, and client notes and intake forms needing to be completed in many work environments, some career counselors feel as though not enough time is allotted for them to amply serve as career counselors. Other career counselors seek to integrate computer-based career interventions or career assessments such as the Myers-Briggs Personality Inventory (MBTI) or the Strong Interest Inventory (SII) but are unable to do so due to financial constraints. Limitations of career resources such as field-specific texts or other career information can be of difficulty to career counselors as well.

A misunderstanding of what career counseling is within an institution is another difficulty that can plague career counselors. For example, many career development professionals at a small liberal arts colleges report that career counseling is at times misunderstood or unappreciated by faculty and administration as well as students. Some believe that the work of a career development professional at a small liberal arts college should focus solely on employer relations and job placement activities for upcoming college graduates. Career counseling, however, opposed to career "case management" should be viewed as an opportunity for client self-discovery and growth rather than simply placing a client in a job.

Career counselor burnout is another issue that career counselors must be sensitive to. Figler and Bowles (1999) offer four helpful and somewhat entertaining indications that a career counselor might be experiencing burnout:

1. *All career counseling clients begin to sound the same*: Where all client's cases seem to melt together, the career counselor forgets who said what, and nothing seems to be getting accomplished;

2. *A more concrete job is beginning to look more appealing to you*: This sometimes happens when career counselors get more interested in the jobs they are helping their clients explore;

3. *You don't want to admit what you do for a living when you're asked at social occasions*;

4. *Your empathy tank is running low.*

In the event a career counselor is experiencing these or other signs of burnout, it is suggested that the counselor seek supervision from another career counselor and consult with other helping professionals. In some cases, the career counselor may need to step away from the work for a period of time to gain perspective and assess whether this is what s/he wants to do.

Rewards of the Work

Despite the difficulties which at times plague career counselors, the work of career counseling is for many an intensely rewarding experience. Many career counselors find fulfillment in helping their clients realize and articulate their values, skills, interests, and personality preferences. In many cases, the outcome of a series of career counseling sessions result in a positive career or job change of a client; this measurable outcome becomes a source of inspiration and joy for both the client and the career counselor.

If one if fortunate to work as a career counselor in an organization made up of other career counselors, the "teamwork" atmosphere can be rewarding and entertaining. Sharing case studies with colleagues helps career counselors to learn and grow. Discovering new resources and texts help to reinvigorate commonly used theories. The sharing of ideas helps to keep career counselors engaged in the therapeutic process and interested in their work. Additionally, career counselors report that they learn more about their own values, interests, skills, personality, decision-making styles, and working styles when working in a team setting.

As you may realize as you explore the chapters of this text, it can be argued that many of the career paths outlined here are variations on a unified theme: the goal of "helping professions" such as social work, counseling, and counseling psychology all aim to positively aid in the growth and development of other human beings. As many of those in the helping professions report, the work of meeting another human being in the midst of their frustration, cynicism, anxiety, or hopelessness and working with that person to unearth the multiple dimensions of reality and begin to see ways to make positive changes in her or his life is an extremely rewarding and liberating experience. Though the work is difficult at times, many career counselors report that the cathartic "a-ha!" moments and help to sustain them and make them ever-thankful to have found a professional identity in the fields of career counseling and career development.

How to Get Started on this Career Track

As suggested earlier in this chapter, "job shadowing" and "informational interviewing" are popular career interventions that provide valuable information on any given career. An easy way for students interested in working in the fields of career counseling and career development is to take the time to meet with a career development professional to learn more about the work.

Howard Figler and Richard N. Bolles (1999) offer an accessible and entertaining introduction to the world of career counseling in *The Career Counselor's Handbook* that serves as a good general introduction. Jane L. Swanson and Nadja A. Fouad (1999) offer a more sophisticated and theoretical introduction to career counseling and career development theory through a series of case studies in *Career theory and practice: Learning through case studies. The role of work in people's lives: Applied career counseling and vocational psychology*, (2005) by Nadene Peterson and Roberto Gonzalez includes some of the most comprehensive analysis of the changing culture of the world of work and how daily work-life is influenced by social, economic, cultural, and educational systems. Many introductory courses in social work and counseling master's-level programs include a course on career counseling or career development and it is not uncommon to find a chapter devoted to career development in an introductory theories course. It is hoped, though, that after reading this chapter, you will not approach the topics of career counseling and career development with apathy and loathing!

There are also a handful of professional associations that one interested in the fields of career counseling and career development should become familiar with. The American Counseling Association (ACA) publishes the *Journal of Counseling and Development* which periodically offers articles on career development theory and practice. *The Career Development Quarterly,* published by the National Career Development Association, offers a wealth of articles on the fields. The *Journal of Social Work Education,* published by the National Association of Social Workers, serves as another source of articles on career counseling and career development.

Further, both the National Association of Social Workers and the National Career Development Association, in cooperation with the American Counseling Association, represent the interests of their members in Washington and lobby members of the Congress. National media frequently consult these organizations which provide leadership and vision to their respective fields. It is not uncommon to hear of the work of these organizations in printed media, radio, and television.

As with any career path, however, the importance of finding a mentor whom you trust and believe in cannot be stressed enough. A mentor can help you to sort out the seemingly obscure research literature or obscure theorists; a mentor can help you to find your place in any given profession. Try to find a mentor that will take the time to know a bit about both your own academic and personal history and who will help you to put the work of theorists and researchers in a context which gives their work meaning and direction. If you are considering a master's-level practicum or internship in career counseling, be sure to check the credentials and professional reputation of your potential supervisor.

L'Invitation au Voyage

This chapter offered a basic outline of the fields of career counseling and career development and hopefully served to give you an introductory view of the work of these fields. It is hoped that you will be able to use this chapter as a beginning resource as you further explore the realms of career counseling and career development.

If you are interested in aiding those searching to find passion and meaning in their work-lives, if you have an interest in work lives and labor market trends, and if you are interested with working with multiple constituents such as clients, employers, hiring organizations, government organizations, etc., you are invited to join in the journey and voyage that is career counseling. The fields of career counseling and career development work with larger disciplines such as sociology, education, theology, psychology, economics, and labor studies, as well as other disciplines where the challenges of day-to-day work are examined and considered.

If you are able to find work that you are passionate about, it is this passion for a career that, in turn, leads to work of quality and clarity. A good career counselor will then help her/his clients to find that passion in their own lives and careers in addition to helping shape culture and the ways that society looks at working life.

As with any career in the helping professions, many which are outlined in this text, one will get out of one's career just as much as one puts into it. There are indeed many paths, but one purpose to aide in the development of those who are struggling to find hope and meaning in their lives. The best of luck to you as you travel on your own vocational journey.

References

Blustein, D.L. (2001). Extending the reach of vocational psychology: Toward an inclusive and integrative psychology of working. *Journal of Vocational Behavior*, 59, 171-182.

DOL. (1998). O*NET (http://www.doleta.gov/programs.onet/) Washington, DC: Author.

Figler, H. & Bolles, R.N. (1999). *The career counselor's handbook*. Berkeley: Ten Speed Press.

Gysbers, N.C., Heppner, M.J.,& Johnson, J.A. (1998). *Career counseling: Process, issues, and techniques*. Needham Heights: Allyn & Bacon.

Iaccarino, G. (2000). Computer-assisted career guidance systems. In *Career counseling of college students: An empirical guide to strategies that work*. Washington, DC: American Psychological Association.

Parsons, F. (1909). *Choosing a vocation*. Boston: Houghton Mifflin International.

Peterson, N. & Gonzalez, R.C. (2005). *The role of work in people's lives: Applied career counseling and vocational psychology* (2nd ed.). Belmont: Thompson Brooks/Cole.

Pope, M. (1995). CCDA leadership: Cultivating the vitality of our profession. *CCDA News*, 11(1), 1, 5. [Original publication].

Pope, M. (1999). Applications of group counseling techniques in Asian cultures. *Journal of Multicultural Counseling and Development*, 27, 18-30.

Pope, M. (2000). A brief history of career counseling in the united states. *The Career Development Quarterly*, 194-211.

Swanson, J.L. & Fouad, N.A. (1999). *Career theory and practice: Learning through case studies*. Thousand Oakes: Sage Publications, Inc.

Whiston, S.C., Sexton, T.L., & Lasoff, D.L. (1998). Career-intervention outcome: A replication an extension of Oliver and Spokane (1988). *Journal of Counseling Psychology*, 45, 150-165.

3

COLLEGE MENTAL HEALTH COUNSELOR

ഇന്ദ്ര

David Weed MA, LMHC
Saint Joseph's College
Rensselaer, Indiana

Nature of the Work

College is both a time and a place—traditionally, it is for students in the four year transition period from adolescence to young adulthood; and, as a place, a college is a unique institution committed to advanced learning. In other words, mental health counseling at a college is closely defined by both the developmental age of the population, between the ages of 18 and 22 years-old, as well as all the typical attributes of a college as particular kind of place. This chapter describes mental health counseling at a small, private, residential, liberal arts college in the Midwest.

Counseling services at such a college are meant to help students manage nearly every aspect of their lives. College students bring with them their unresolved adolescent problems as they continue to construct an autonomous self, and unfortunately, some are also challenged in this period of transition by the emergence of significantly disabling mental disorders. Therefore, a mental health counselor at any post-secondary school will eventually work with all the developmental issues of this age group, as well as the full range of psychopathology.

Adolescence and young adulthood are periods in which the symptoms of many acute and chronic conditions first appear—mood disorders, the wide spectrum of anxiety disorders, and psychotic disorders all may emerge for the first time during college years. At the same time, the uncertainties and transitions of life also become more evident to college students, leaving them increasingly vulnerable to adjustment disorders, substance-related disorders, eating disorders, and sleep disorders. Residential college students also live in a newly demanding social context of novel freedoms and opportunities of choice while concurrently they are increasingly less likely to be grounded in the familiar moral certainties that once guided their earlier years.

College counseling services report that today's undergraduates appear to be more anxious than previous generations of such students, and that they are far more likely to appear in a counseling center already experienced in previous counseling. They are also more likely to be using prescribed psychotropic medications. Counselors report that these students are presenting with elevated levels of distress and are diagnosed with more severe disabilities than previously.

Even though these are not typical years for most chronic health problems, distressed and stressed college students often seem far less healthy than one would otherwise expect. Sleep is challenged, and nutrition is sketchy during college. While studies show that college students talk the talk, they badly fail at walking a healthy walk. Although these well-informed folks understand health issues, they do not apply much of their knowledge—college can be a time and place for binge drinking, cigarette smoking, unprotected sex, and drug experimentation.

Sexual opportunities open up for this group, applying immense and dramatic pressure on this intense life experience. Sexual activity without emotional intimacy has become a norm for many of these students. The "random hookup" scene seems to guarantee concentrated sexual passion totally outside any emotional relationship. Students who spend a few sexual hours together while drinking, then find it awkward meeting their interim partner in class the next morning.

Although today's students seem to be affected more deeply by the stresses of their lives, they also remain ideal candidates for counseling as they are young and intelligent—they typically bring good insight into self-discovery and self-management. Psychoanalysts have used the acronym YAVIS to describe the ideal therapy client as Young, Attractive, Verbal,

Intelligent, and Successful—good descriptors of many college students. Unless they are disabled by a severe Axis II personality disorder, or are overwhelmed by an Axis I disorder of major proportions, college students often respond rapidly to psychotherapy.

Even though the students are often ideal clients, providing concentrated, uninterrupted psychological services to them can be seriously problematic at colleges. For example, college psychotherapy is defined more by the academic calendar than it is by just about any other variable. Semesters, holidays, and summer breaks shape the therapeutic environment along with the varying intensity of academic life; all-night study for exams alternates with the abandon of party nights. Athletic practices and competitions both at home and on the road break up the therapy schedule. Providing sufficient therapeutic resources to students can also be problematic, especially at those schools that have limited finances and personnel to invest in supportive student development resources. Recent financial pressures at most colleges mean that student services such as counseling now have smaller budgets; this can mean that counselors need to limit the number of sessions provided to an individual, and that brief therapy will be the only viable service model.

Gratefully, brief therapies have produced effective approaches to working with both the developmental issues and the mental disorders of college students. Brief therapies appear significantly successful in counseling service outcomes studies. Even single session counseling has been demonstrated to be useful, an important fact as one session is often the modal number of sessions at a college counseling center, while the mean number of sessions is often around six or seven; fifteen sessions—one semester - is a common top limit to direct services.

Along with providing individual psychotherapy, a college counselor will also be expected to be competent in other treatment modalities and in providing other services. Group work is common at larger colleges and could include group therapy, support groups, and educational groups. Outreach work by counselors can be important, and counselors are often asked to provide preventative and educational programming, both in the center and in residence halls. Consultation to parents, faculty and college staff is yet another important aspect of the work.

Some schools provide counseling mandated by the college judicial system, while others are philosophically opposed to that kind of service. This is still a hotly debated issue among counseling center directors. Some see mandated counseling as a rare opportunity to reach those students who would not seek counseling on their own, but who are often the ones most in need of it. Others see mandated counseling as an oxymoron: is it really "counseling" if you are forced to attend sessions? Further, doubters of judicially mandated counseling ask if the counseling service could eventually be perceived by students as an extension of the judicial system rather than an independent and objective agency within the college.

College counseling services are also sometimes required to review learning disability documentation provided by students who are seeking special educational accommodations based on their disabilities. This requires the clinician to become familiar with the Americans with Disabilities Act (ADA) and to become competent at analyzing the supporting data brought forward by such students. Attention-Deficit/Hyperactivity Disorder (AD/HD) and other clinical conditions may also be cited by some students seeking special educational accommodations.

Career counseling is a major offering of some counseling services. As a future vocational life looms nearer on the horizon for college students, it may be near enough to impinge uncomfortably on many of their educational decisions. Dreams, fantasies, and tentative notions of a distant life are now crowded into the harsh reality of a parental question: "What are you going to do with a major in…?"

College counselors need to make referrals for psychiatric evaluations, and most counselors will be required to provide crisis interventions. It is typical for counselors to rotate through a 24-hour on-call system to provide a professional response to psychological emergencies.

Training and Degree(s) Required

Joining a college counseling service will require a level of education, training, and experience that will attract the attention of a Counseling Director who ordinarily hires Ph.D. and Psy.D. Counseling or Clinical Psychologists, professionals who have completed a year-long American Psychological Association internship, and possibly have carried out post-doctoral work as well. Competition for college counseling positions is intense because so many professionals are attracted to the stability and benefits offered by colleges where they will not need to contend with third-party billing and the treatment restrictions imposed by managed care systems. However, progressively smaller budgets at colleges now make it increasingly financially attractive to hire master's level practitioners who do not command the highest salaries.

An annual survey of 333 American colleges and universities show that a newly hired M.S.W. without prior experience would be paid a salary in a range of $32 to $37,000; while a M.S.W. with considerable college counseling experience, can earn a salary that is substantially higher—one salary for 2003 is reported at $65,000. The salaries commanded by experienced master's level clinicians can eventually match that of new doctoral counselors. This author's graduate education is limited to a M.A. in Counseling Psychology, and was hired as a director with a salary that matches that of a counselor with a new doctorate. The mean salary of a counseling service director in 2003 was $68,500, while the range of salaries varied wildly from $30,000 to $120,000!

Anyone wishing to eventually practice in a college counseling service needs to be dedicated to achieving academic excellence and to engaging in rigorous training. Education should be as narrowly focused on college/university counseling as the degree program will allow, with all practica and internships demonstrating a thorough exposure to working with this age group in post-secondary institutions. Comments by professors, training instructors, and supervisors must demonstrate a high level of clinical competency, personal maturity, and a demonstrated ability to work particularly well with this population.

National certification is useful, and state licensure will be required; and, while certification is not difficult to acquire—normally directly after graduation—sitting for a mental health licensure exam requires the accumulation of many hours (about three years worth) of post-graduate direct service and supervision.

Personality Traits Important to Succeed

Nearly all authorities on the subject now agree that a sound therapeutic relationship is the fundamental attribute of all effective counseling, no matter what modality is used, no matter which theoretical orientation guides the practitioner. A sound therapeutic relationship in itself may not be sufficient, but it is necessary; without it, psychotherapy can be mechanical and unconvincing. All counseling professionals must come to terms with their own ability to relate well with clients who are in pain, and who are possibly disorganized, poorly contained, overly demanding, and inappropriate in their behavior.

Theorists and educators have written and taught extensively about the personal characteristics that strengthen the therapeutic relationship and efficacy of counseling. These writers and teachers have pointed to the fact that we will be most able to promote healthful change in others if we have progressed well in our own development. An effective counselor is sure to have spent much time and effort in self examination, and in developing ways to progressively construct a professional persona with whom clients may easily engage at deep levels of intimate interaction.

But beyond the personality characteristics expected of all generalist counselors, are those that facilitate work with this special population of age and place—after all, college counselors must thoroughly enjoy college students, and they must also enjoy working in academia. While residential college students live lives that are quite different from non-students of the same age, many argue that the same is true of college faculty and administrators. Professors have vocational lives dedicated to advanced levels of learning and teaching, while college administrators mange the total institutional context that makes learning and teaching possible. Counselors need to know how to work well with these kinds of colleagues.

While it is important that a college counselor enjoy working with young adults, it is equally important that the counselor is one who has successfully negotiated the transitions of this stage, and is not attracted to college counseling as a process of self-development by proxy. A college counselor needs to be certain that he or she is appropriately attracted to the counseling concerns of students, while also able to maintain appropriate boundaries. Over-affiliation with students obviously ends in a marked reduction in the therapeutic distance required in a sound counseling relationship.

At the other end of such a spectrum would be counselors who are unable to work effectively with students because they are overly committed to a role that is perceived by students as parental or authoritarian. Mental health professionals who are prone to substituting advice giving and directive guidance for counseling will not succeed with college students—college students are particularly adept at distinguishing caring encouragement in self-exploration from efforts at covert moralizing.

Difficulties of the Work

Both the difficulties and the rewards of this work are a function of the two aspects of college counseling: college students as a special population, and the college as a particular kind of place. College students live lives that are distinctly different from non-student cohorts, and these differences contribute to both the difficulties and the rewards of working with them.

And because colleges are unlike most other institutions, working at a college brings particular frustrations and some attractive opportunities.

A difficulty often experienced by college counselors is that of working in a professional context that is infamous for its petty politics and territoriality. Colleges are well known for their harboring of administrators and faculty members that are as insular and narrow in their outlooks as they are intelligent and accomplished. It appears that gathering advanced degrees is in itself not sufficient to guarantee openness and collegiality.

Those of us who work in colleges were often originally shocked to learn that we would face such fierce departmental rivalries and personal defensiveness. However much we might wish that it were otherwise, we experience repeatedly the fact that some very intelligent people can behave very badly, or at least, very self-protectively. One of the first tasks of working in these unique institutions is to come to terms with the fact that one will sometimes be held in high suspicion by others, and will need to learn how to be politically effective in such a climate.

It often seems that the role of college counselors, and college counseling services, are often misunderstood by parents, faculty, athletic coaches and administrative staff. It feels, sometimes, that our work is either over-valued and held to impossible standards of helpfulness ("Make my anorexic daughter healthy by the end of the semester!"), or devalued as wholly unproductive ("After three sessions with you, my depressed advisee is *still* not getting good grades!"). Administrators can expect us to accurately predict very ambiguous future behaviors by students ("Are you absolutely certain that this student will not commit suicide and is safe to live on campus?"). We are sometimes treated as if we have special insights into the human condition ("You're a counselor, tell me why people behave like this?"), while parents often fear we identify too completely with an unhappy son or daughter ("You probably blame the parents for the student's poor behavior, don't you?").

Six years after establishing a mental health counseling service at a small college, this author still is approached by faculty who believe that the counselor's role is to advise students on appropriate coursework as well as tell them how best to get along well in life—some variation of "You have to give it a hundred and ten percent!" The student admissions guides, who bring prospective students through Counseling Services as part of their campus tour, invariably tell the prospectives and their parents that "Counseling is for students who have problems with their roommates!"

College students are as prone as any to swallowing whole the pop psychology produced by mass media advice pundits who appear to have co-opted the world of psychotherapy and counseling, leaving practitioners often feeling badly misunderstood. Students, parents, and administrators who do not have counseling educations often develop very simplistic ideas about what counseling is or should be. Developing sensible counseling service policies can be slowed by the need to educate others about particular problems such as eating disorders or self-injury.

Counseling confidentiality is a particularly thorny issue on college campuses: parents are stunned to learn they must not expect to learn confidential information about their son or daughter from a counselor; a well-meaning faculty member automatically assumes a counselor would at least confirm the fact that a student is or is not engaged in counseling; college administrators can sometimes accuse a counselor of not being a team-player when that counselor refuses to divulge private information about a student; even the college health service staff can feel that counseling records ought to be automatically open to medical practitioners there.

It is difficult to overstress this particular difficulty. Small colleges are communities in which rumors are easily created and maintained, and establishing a reputation with students as being absolutely trustworthy is nearly the paramount task of counseling service directors. Directors have learned that their centers will live or die by the level of trust students have in their counseling confidentiality.

Dual relationships are particularly difficult to avoid on small college campuses where the counselor may be expected to serve in a variety of roles. Counselors, like other members of the college staff, may be asked to take on such roles as advising student organizations, leading freshman seminar groups, or even teaching a class. Such roles could (and sometimes must) compromise the role of the counselor, placing the counselor in an impossible ethical and professional conflict. Administrators and members of the faculty often end up questioning why the counselor seems to be so touchy about such issues, and the counselor may end up labeled as "uncooperative" and "a loner" for refusing roles that compromise the counselor's avoidance of judgmental relationships with students who may be, or may become, clients.

Something as simple as a counselor eating in the student cafeteria can become a treatment-relationship issue if an eating disordered client sees the counselor and wonders if the counselor has observed her eating. Students may also attempt to manipulate a counselor into agreeing to intervene inappropriately in other realms of the student's college life. Many counselors, for example, have had the experience of a client requesting the counselor tell the housing staff that the student needs a special type of housing because of particular psychological issues.

Because college counseling is largely a generalist counseling career track, this can bring its own discomforts: stretching to be at least minimally effective in so many different areas of problematic behavior. Large centers may have specialists in such areas as addictions, eating disorders, and multicultural counseling, but small college counseling services need to rely on the ability of the counselor to acquire and maintain at least moderately high levels of competence in all possible areas. For some, this can be an exciting challenge rather than a major problem; but, however it is experienced by the counselor, being called on to meet such a wide array of issues does demand a continuous life of keeping current with the treatment literature.

Rewards of the Work

College counseling services are often intellectually stimulating places to work. As stated above, whether a counseling generalist or one who has a specialty, the college counselor will usually be expected to remain professionally alert to the advances in the sciences supporting psychotherapies. For those who relish continuous professional education, college counseling services can be wonderfully supportive of professional development and research. Most college counselors will find active encouragement from supervisors to investigate counseling topics, collect and analyze data, write on the subject, and present the resulting research at in-service training sessions or at professional conferences.

College counseling services can also be counselor training sites that bring in an on-going turnover of student trainees and interns. These younger and fresher beginner professionals bring welcome new energy and enthusiasm along with recent exposure to graduate school coursework. Their eagerness and up-to-date education often energizes the counseling service regulars who are prone to become ever more dedicated to what they already know—training sites tend to be intellectually lively.

A client's readiness for change is often seen as one of the primary indicators of success in therapy—college students are at an age where they often *want* to make changes in their lives, and they are living in an educational context that *expects them to change*. In general, college students seeking treatment services are apt to have arrived at their own conclusion that things are not going well in important ways, and they are therefore arriving at the counseling center with a high level of readiness.

As a practitioner most comfortable with cognitive-behavioral therapy, I find working at a college particularly rewarding. For college students, it seems a natural extension of intellect and pragmatism to work within the highly active and cooperative context of cognitive-behavioral therapy; homework, after all, is familiar and expected; closely reasoned thinking, rational discourse, and careful observation of experiences are all fostered in the educational world they live in. Students experience the Socratic method in the classroom, and are therefore not too surprised to experience this type of dialog in the counseling session.

"Biblio-therapy" is a common adjunct to counseling sessions in college centers. Students read large quantities of educational materials and primary sources in college. It is therefore easy for the student client to experience counseling reading assignments as an obvious supplement to the experiential learning of the counseling session.

Obviously, for those of us who understand therapy as essentially a learning experience, there is a wonderful synergy involved with providing powerful therapy experiences within the context of a life focused on learning. Liberal arts colleges base their curricula on the general understanding that the educational mission is, after all, to be "liberating." Counseling, therefore, can be understood and experienced as an extension of the students' larger educational life.

Another very positive aspect of college counseling is its cost: it is either free or comparably very inexpensive. This author works at an institution that presently provides four years (or more) of unlimited counseling sessions, and does so without any charges beyond the general fees charged all students. There are, however, more and more colleges that are experimenting with fee-for-service models to help compensate for the rising operating costs with which colleges are now faced. The typical fees charged students by those schools are very modest compared to private practice rates.

How to Get Started on this Career Track

As described earlier, getting started in college counseling is easiest when the counseling student knows far in advance that this is his or her goal. When college counseling is known to be a person's ultimate vocational track, the student can design the entire educational enterprise in ways that will most ensure this. Even at the undergraduate level, coursework and experiential opportunities can be sought that will best lead to eventual jobs in colleges and universities.

To find out if one is interested in, and suitable for, college counseling, the potential counselor should visit college counseling services and seek conversations with those who work there. Counseling Services directors, training directors, and counselors will all most likely be quite accommodating to those who are seeking a better understanding of college counseling as a career. They will be in a good position to advise a person new to the whole range of counseling possibilities.

This author gained a liberal arts degree in the humanities, and included two upper-level undergraduate classes in counseling theory and practice. This was followed by a two-year, 63-credit M.A. degree in Counseling Psychology that included two academic- year-long internships: the first at a private college preparatory school, and the second in a college counseling service. A two-year postgraduate internship at another college counseling service was followed by a post as a staff counselor at the same college. The internship and the staff position provided the supervised counseling hours required for the licensing exam. The author was then offered a directorship at the school where he now works.

4

SOCIAL WORK CAREER PATH AS A CLINIC DIRECTOR AND THERAPIST

ഇഇരു

Cathy Ticen, MA, LMHC
Wabash Valley Hospital
Rensselaer, Indiana

Nature of the Work

During a recent Career Day presentation, a student asked me, "What is a typical day like for you at Wabash Valley Hospital?" I found myself laughing on the inside (not outwardly...I exercised good impulse control) because there is no such thing as a "typical day" in a rural mental health clinic. My staff often comments that it feels like we work in an emergency room. Their description is really very accurate. In a rural community, resources are limited. Multiple external agencies rely on our clinic to assist them with difficult situations by providing crisis intervention, treatment, consultation, and training services. For example, our clinic is routinely asked by the local county hospital to provide psychological consults. Our clinicians in the ER, ICU, or on the general medical floor do these consults on-site. The goal is to assess the mental status of the patient and make treatment recommendations to the attending physician. The local schools, Crisis Center, jail, pastors, and police officers also request similar crisis intervention services from us. It is the presence of emergencies, which adds the most variety to our daily clinical routines. We are required to provide immediate crisis care to anyone who presents as suicidal or homicidal. When a crisis call comes, all routine services come to a halt for the clinician who is asked to handle the situation. This means paperwork is put on hold, regular clients may have to be rescheduled, and therapy sessions may need to be interrupted. Fortunately, not all services requested by our community are crisis-focused. External agencies also request training and consultation services. Providing this service ends up benefiting both our clinic and the requesting agency. For example, I have provided crisis intervention training and/or materials to the local college, police departments, pastors, hospital, and schools. This training helps external agencies to recognize and manage crises in a way that facilitates teamwork with a clinician as opposed to making our jobs more difficult. Delivering the aforementioned services is energizing, but can also be overwhelming at times. The needs of both the clients and the community are extensive. As a result, the treatment team has to be able to multi-task and be flexible in order to meet the demands for service.

The clinic environment is fast-paced the majority of the time. I find myself juggling hats back and forth constantly between my supervisory and clinical roles. I supervise five therapists, three case managers, four secretaries, and two psychiatrists. In the supervisory role I have to make sure that my staff is providing quality care and completing paperwork in a timely manner. The staff has certain agency standards that they are required to meet. Other external sources like insurance companies, state and federal guidelines, accreditation bodies, etc., shape these agency standards. There are a lot of rules for the staff to remember and meet. Monitoring staff compliance in these areas requires chart reviews, clinical supervision, performance evaluations, and staff meetings. The Clinic Director's role also involves troubleshooting. If a problem arises between staff, with clients or with external agencies, it is my responsibility to fix it. The Director role also involves marketing, interagency collaboration, attending system-wide meetings, and completing special projects assigned by the CEO of our hospital.

The clinical side of my position is intricately interwoven and performed concurrently with my administrative responsibilities. I provide direct client care, which includes services like crisis intervention, therapy (individual, group, and family), and associated case management services that support therapeutic interventions. Beyond direct client contact, my clinical role includes supportive services like interagency collaboration, case conferences, interdisciplinary staffings, and paperwork completion. The paperwork portion of being a clinician is labor-intensive and often more challenging than the actual client contact itself. When a client comes in for services, I have to write a biopsychosocial assessment, treatment plan, mental status, demographic forms, diagnosis sheet, and state-based functional assessment (where applicable). The paperwork requirements of the initial clinical session actually involves more time than the direct client contact itself. After the initial client contact, the paperwork involves progress notes at each session, updating treatment plans, updating biopsychosocial summaries annually, completing state functional assessment reviews approximately every six months, submitting reports to external agencies, and completing forms required by insurance companies. Although there are a lot of tasks to complete each day, the exciting part is that the work is never dull. Time flies by quickly and the rewards are numerous. In my opinion, being a supervisor and a clinician is the best of both worlds. The experiences I've had in this position are priceless.

Training and Degrees Required

In order to be eligible for my current position, I had to have a minimum of a Master's degree in either counseling or social work. In addition, I had to be eligible for licensure or hold a valid license to perform therapy in the state of Indiana. Although I currently am a licensed mental health counselor, I did not start out at Wabash Valley with all of this in place. I obtained both my undergraduate and Master's degrees from Ball State University. In order to be eligible for licensure, I had to be involved in a CACREP approved counseling psychology program and complete a minimum of sixty credit hours of counseling course work. In addition, I had to complete a 100-hour practicum, a 600-hour clinical internship, and have 2000 hours of supervised clinical experience. Last, I had to pass a national exam acceptable to the Health Professions Bureau. Licensure did not come into existence in the state of Indiana until after I had completed my Master's degree. As a result, I was able to be "grandfathered" into licensure by proving that I had met the aforementioned requirements. In terms of the national examination requirements, I took two written exams (NCC-National Certified Counseling Exam and ICAADA-Indiana Counselors Association on Alcohol and Drug Abuse) and one oral examination (for ICAADA). For actual licensure, only the NCC exam was required. Now that I have obtained licensure, I have to complete twenty hours of continuing education per year and maintain privileging requirements with both Wabash Valley and Jasper County Hospitals. To have privileges to practice with Wabash Valley Hospital, I have to maintain licensure, complete continuing education requirements, and submit to chart reviews in each of my areas of practice. In my case, I hold privileges for working with SMI (seriously mentally ill adults), SED (seriously emotionally disturbed children and adolescents), and SA (substance abuse). I also have to maintain requirements for individual, group, and family therapy along with assessment privileges.

Personality Traits and Skills Deemed
Important to Succeed

During the course of my career, I have watched people both flourish and burnout in this field. It seems that the clinicians who flourish in this field have good time management skills, remain calm in crisis, work well with the rest of the clinical team, possess strong organizational skills, maintain boundaries, practice good self-care, communicate well, and relate well with people. As previously noted, this is a fast-paced and demanding field. If a clinician is not able to be calm in the face of a crisis, he or she will probably not last in a clinical setting like ours. We deal with multiple emergencies and may receive a call at any time day or night. Related to this, the clinician needs to know when to ask for help and then reach out for the same on a regular basis. Working well with other staff in a community mental health center is essential. Trying to handle cases solo is a recipe for disaster. In addition, it is vital to be able to maintain boundaries (leave clinical issues at work), practice good self-care, and manage stress well. On any given day, a clinician may handle crises as well as several hours worth of routine therapy sessions along with associate paperwork. If a clinician is unable to leave client problems at work, he or she will become overwhelmed and be at risk for burnout. The clinician also needs to practice the same skills we teach our clients like getting adequate rest, eating well, and dealing with problems as they come up. An inability to do these things also puts a clinician at risk for burnout. Lastly, the clinician needs to possess strong time management and organizational skills. Juggling a full day of clients and the associated paperwork can be overwhelming. If a clinician gets behind, it can be very difficult to catch up and to meet standards. Therefore, it is important for a clinician to know how to prioritize tasks, structure time, and develop strategies to meet agency standards. In terms of the supervisory role, all of the aforementioned skills are vitally important. The supervisor needs the added skills of problem-solving, remaining objective in staff situations, resolving conflict, and dealing with the difficult people.

Difficulties of the Work

Although this position is very rewarding, there are some factors that can be difficult to manage. A lot of these challenges have already been described above like competing demands, high expectations/standards, paperwork overload, frequent interruptions to handle crises, and juggling roles. In addition to these difficulties, there are a couple of other challenges to watch out for, especially in rural mental health care. One of the challenges in a rural community is that a clinician tends to run into his or her clients on a regular basis outside of work. In a rural area, there are very few activities and limited shopping areas available. I run into clients at the grocery, the doctor's office, church, community events, etc. To cope with this challenge, I talk with clients early into their course of therapy about confidentiality and boundaries. To prepare them for the possibility of running into me outside of the clinic, I talk with them about how my role is different at that point. I will not approach them but will say "hi" if they initiate a greeting. I emphasize that we cannot discuss therapeutic issues while in the community and they need to call between sessions if they need assistance. I also stress that I will not be sharing with anyone about if or how I know him or her. This proactive step with clients has prevented a lot of problems for me in my clinical practice. Before I took this step with clients there were times when they were offended because I didn't talk to them at the grocery store. Some were also worried that other people might find out that they go to see a therapist. Beyond the spontaneous meetings, another challenge of rural mental health care is the lack of community resources. We have clients or transients that walk in off the street and beg us to help them find food, shelter, and/or transportation. We do not have a homeless shelter in our community. Transportation services are very limited and only run during normal business hours. It is difficult to turn people away when it is cold outside.

In addition there are people who have learned to "work the system" by saying things like "If I threaten to kill myself, then you will have to put me inpatient, right?" Our treatment team relies heavily on the local ministerial association to assist us with cases like this, but their resources are also limited as well. As a result, clinicians have to be creative and reach out to other agencies for assistance. Juggling all of these competing demands, feelings, and needs is probably the most difficult part of being a clinic director/therapist.

Rewards of the Work

I have heard clinicians comment at times something to the effect of, "Tell me why it is that we do what we do? Why do we keep getting up every morning and tackling seemingly insurmountable situations?" Basically there are times when a clinician may wonder why it's worth it. During the times when I feel discouraged, I look around my office and remember the mile markers of success on this journey of therapy. Some of these reminders are tangible. During play therapy, some of my young clients have drawn me pictures or made me cards. The cards will say things like, "I love you because you help me and don't hurt me." Looking at these handmade expressions of gratitude restores my passion for helping people get better. As I hold these drawings, I picture scenes of transformation that I see in the eyes of both children and adults alike. It has been said that the eyes are the windows of the soul. This saying is so true. I am humbled by the privilege I have to gaze into the eyes of someone's soul and help them to walk the journey from pain to healing. When eyes that are clouded by pain begin to sparkle with life-sustaining joy again, I remember why I sit in this chair each day as a therapist. Even seemingly small steps of progress, to me, are cause for great celebration. Most of the rewards are captured via observation, but occasionally they are overt. There will be times that a client will call out of the blue and say, "I just wanted to thank you for helping me. You changed my life." Those times, although they are rare, restore my passion as well.

Last, I find it energizing to be a part of interagency collaboration. It is not an easy task to build or maintain those networks. However, it is highly rewarding when the community can work together as a team to help a client. I have been in crisis intervention situations where several different agencies pitched in to use their strengths and resources to help the client. Interdisciplinary collaboration is rewarding on both supervisory and clinical levels. Overall, I wouldn't want to give up this chair for anything. To walk alongside people in their journey of healing is rewarding beyond what words can express. Challenges fade into the background as healing occurs.

How to Get Started on this Career Track

When I participate in Career Days at the local high schools, the question of how to get started inevitably comes up. What I recommend first is that people do some research. Read about and/or talk to someone who is in the field. If at all possible, do some job shadowing. Confidentiality laws complicate access here, but there are some situations where it may be feasible to at least tour a community mental health center and talk with the staff. If you are still drawn to the field after taking this step, I highly recommend doing some career testing. It is important to make sure you have the skills and personality type which matches this kind of a position. Interest inventories will help you sort out what occupations best fit your personality and skill base. If your skills and interest areas match the field, then pursue the coursework. Talk with your advisor about what courses are needed to obtain the degree. If volunteer work is possible, take advantage of these opportunities. Firsthand experience will help you to make the decision if this field is right for you or not. This experience also helps you to develop valuable skills, which will be later used in the field. If possible, obtain a mentor. Choose someone who is already active in the field who can guide you through the process of obtaining a degree, securing licensure, and finding employment. Last, find support people who will help you manage your stress along the way. Burnout is a very real problem in helping professions. It can destroy a clinician's passion for the field. Having a solid support network that can hold you accountable to dealing with your own stress will prevent burnout when you are in the field.

5

SOCIAL WORK DEAN

ഇരു

Santos Hernandez, PhD

There are a variety of careers one can pursue with a background in social work. Among these is a career in higher education as a social work faculty member. There is also the opportunity within higher education to become an administrator in charge of social work education programs by serving as a Dean or Director. In social work education, degree programs are either housed, or nested, within other academic units, such as a college, or they are stand-alone programs, such as a school. When programs are nested within other colleges they are either programs or departments and are headed by a Director. When programs are stand-alone, as in a school or college of social work, a Dean heads them.

A Dean is considered the chief administrative officer of the social work education program. Typically a college or school of social work houses a graduate program that offers the Master of Social Work (M.S.W.) degree and may also house an undergraduate program which offers a Bachelor in Social Work (B.S.W.) degree. Schools may also house a Doctoral program in social work leading to a Ph.D. or D.S.W. in social work. In 2003, there were approximately 177 Master's programs (either accredited or in candidacy), 455 B.S.W. programs, and approximately 90 Ph.D. programs in social work. (CSWE, Reporter, 2003)

Most job descriptions for the position of Dean read something like:

The Dean serves as the Chief Administrative Officer of the school and provides administrative and educational leadership to the school. Duties and responsibilities of the Dean include, but are not limited to:

1. General administration and management of school functions;

2. Establish and maintain policies of the school and university;

3. Responsible for the hiring, supervision, and evaluation of faculty and staff;

4. Direct faculty in curriculum development and coordination;

5. Responsible for fiscal management of internal and grant/contract generated funds;

6. Responsible for fundraising and advancement efforts for the school;

7. Supervises key administrative staff personnel;

8. Serve on Council of Deans and other academic committees of the university;

9. Ex-Officio member of all school faculty committees;

10. Develop and maintain community and professional relations;

11. Maintain accreditation standards.

Most advertisements for the position of Dean read something like:

The Dean will be expected to build an environment of support and innovation while further advancing the stature of the school's academic programs. The Dean will be an energetic, experienced social work professional with vision, creativity, and a willingness to take risks. He or she must be a proven administrator with a track record of working collaboratively with a diverse group of faculty and fellow Deans, as well as social agencies and the social work community. The Dean will also have the organizational skills and ability necessary to navigate effectively in a complex academic setting.

The Dean is responsible for the school's general academic and administrative management including curriculum, faculty, resource and program development, and community relations. The Dean will promote high-quality teaching and academic programs as well as research and service related activities.

The successful candidate will have the ability to collaborate with an active collection of scholars in the effort to conduct research, obtain external funding support, publish research, infuse their teaching with the implications of such research, and provide service to the region and the nation.

Each of the above scenarios describes lofty and ambitious expectations for the position of Dean. In addition, higher education in itself is frequently froth with changing expectations and challenges; academia and academic administration are changing both in their complexity and the diverse nature of stakeholder constituencies. Thus, an effective administrator must be adaptive while providing a consistency of vision and direction. The Dean, in particular, must possess the ability to work collaboratively with faculty and administrators while fostering a commitment to enhancing academic and scholastic excellence. Developing strong relations with faculty, exhibiting respect for faculty governance, and fostering interdisciplinary collaborations across the campus will be important in moving any school forward.

Nature of the Work

The nature of being a Dean of a school of social work is in many ways similar to that of an executive administrator of any organization. The skills and competencies involved are fundamental management and leadership, the same as in any other system. Deans, like other administrators, are responsible for the various management functions which are part of the administrative process: planning, implementing, controlling, budgeting, hiring, evaluating and rewarding personnel, fundraising, resource development, and evaluation. The management side of administration is, in part, technical competence and, in part, interpersonal skill. It is therefore important to understand the uniqueness of the academic setting in which higher education administration occurs. In this sense, an academic administrator is uniquely defined by the institutional context and organizational values within which such administration occurs.

Bergquist (1992) describes higher education as encompassing what he calls the four cultures of the academy: a collegial culture, a managerial culture, a developmental culture, and a negotiating culture. Each serves to ascribe meaning to the participants (faculty, students, staff, administrators) within the institutional setting, and provide often-contending values and dynamics within which a Dean, or other administrator, must navigate. Each of these cultures is not mutually exclusive of the others, occurs simultaneously with the others, and will vie for primacy.

The collegial culture:

> ...finds meaning primarily in the disciplines represented by the faculty in the institution. This culture values faculty research and scholarship and the quasi-political governance processes of the faculty; holds untested assumptions about the dominance of rationality in the institution; and conceives of the institution's enterprise as the generation, interpretation, and dissemination of knowledge and as the development of specific values and qualities of character among young men and women who are future leaders of our society. (Bergquist, pp. 4-5)

The managerial culture:

> ...finds meaning primarily in the organization, implementation, and evaluation of work that is directed toward specified goals and purposes. This culture values fiscal responsibility and effective supervisory skills; holds untested assumptions about the capacity of the institution to define and measure its goals and objectives clearly; and conceives of the institution's enterprise as the inculcation of specific knowledge, skills, and attitudes in students so that they might become successful and responsible citizens. (Bergquist, p. 5)

The developmental culture

> ...finds meaning primarily in the creation of programs and activities furthering the personal and professional growth of all members of the collegiate community. This culture values personal openness and service to others, as well as systematic institutional research and curricular planning; holds untested assumptions about the inherent desire of all men and women to attain their own personal maturation, while helping others in the institution become more mature; and conceives of the institution's enterprise as the encouragement of potential for cognitive, affective, and behavioral maturation among all students, faculty, administrators, and staff. (Bergquist, p. 5)

The negotiating culture:

> ...finds meaning primarily in the establishment of equitable and egalitarian policies and procedures for the distribution of resources and benefits in the institution. This culture values confrontation and fair bargaining among constituencies (primarily management and faculty or staff) with vested interests that are inherently in opposition; holds untested assumptions about the ultimate role of power and the frequent need for outside mediation in a viable collegiate institution; and conceives of the institution's enterprise as either the undesirable promulgation of existing (and often repressive) social attitudes and structures or the establishment of new and more liberating social attitudes and structures. (Bergquist, pp. 5-6)

In order to be successful, a Dean must be able to engender the trust and confidence of faculty, staff, students, and other university stakeholders across these four cultures. Bergquist's cultures embody specific expectations of administrative leadership in academia that Deans must in some fashion respond to. Among these are integrity, leadership and management skills, respect for faculty governance and autonomy, effectively transacting with diverse stakeholders, advocating for the academic unit, interpreting organizational needs and aspirations to the task environment (Weinback, 1994), and building a common mission and vision (Kotter, 1996).

Several leadership theorists espouse that integrity is an essential component of leadership (Badaracco, 2002; Bennis, 1997; Bennis and Nanus, 1985; Covey, 1989; Daniels, 1994; Hackman and Johnson, 1991; McCauley, Moxley and Van Velsor, 1998). Core to the issue of integrity is the concept of being an integrated whole. The effective Dean must be able to demonstrate a general consistency in his or her approach to administration and leadership, which in turn will inspire a sense of consistency from those he or she is entrusted to lead. This consistency fosters a sense of trustworthiness and character such that the Dean can be seen as someone to be trusted and who places importance on the best interests of the school in his or her decision-making. Fundamentally, the effective administrator must be seen as an honest person with a strong moral commitment to the work they do. In a very real sense, positions of authority and responsibility are also positions of public trust.

Leadership and management skills are not synonymous, but both are important to the work of academic administration. Bennis and Nanus (1985) suggest, "Managers are people who do things right, leaders are people who do the right thing." In this scheme, managers are problem-solvers focused on organizational stability, physical resources, and efficiency; leaders are problem-solvers focused on managing change, crisis, innovation, spiritual and emotional resources, and organizational effectiveness. Hackman & Johnson, (1991) aptly opine, "Many institutions are very well managed, but very poorly led."

Leadership is a process that is interactive, transactional, and reciprocal, often defined more by "followers" than by the leader...Effective leaders and managers "bring out the best" in others because they look for the best in others (Hackman & Johnson, 1991).

Effective leadership requires sufficient adaptability to fit one's leadership style with the dynamic needs of the organization over time. To be effective over time, leaders must be adaptable to the changing needs of the organization, individuals within that organization, and the demands of the task environment. Universities and schools, like other organizations, are never stagnant. Change is ever-present as the organization responds to changing dynamics among its stakeholder environments. Organizations also experience a cyclical developmental lifespan and will have different leadership needs depending on their stage of development. As a school matures with a core complement of senior faculty, its leadership needs are quite different from one whose faculty have retired out and are replaced with a generation of faculty newer to academia. In the former culture, with an abundance of senior faculty, it is common for the organization to have established ways of doing things that may require little direction from the Dean. But by the same token, this established way of doing things might cause faculty to be resistant to changes in leadership priorities. The latter case of the relatively new generation of faculty might require a higher need for direction and operational engagement from the Dean. Even within these cultures, individual faculty will be at their own unique stage of professional development and have differing leadership needs from administration.

Because the academic culture has evolved over the years to include a high regard for academic freedom and faculty self-governance, the effective Dean must have a sincere respect for faculty governance and autonomy. The faculty culture is highly independent and individualistic. The freedom to pursue one's academic interest is one of the things that make the academic life appealing to many. Such a culture at times contends with management's aim of creating uniformity in collective organization. This creates a need for the administrator to lead through influence and persuasion and to develop inclusive, participatory management styles that are more consistent with a culture of self-governance and autonomy.

It is not enough to understand and appreciate the value orientations and dynamics involved in Bergquist's four cultures; Deans must be able to demonstrate that they can effectively transact the cultures of the academy. Administration is more than just planning and budget management: effective administration involves building effective relationships and alliances with key stakeholders. Chief among these stakeholders are students, faculty, and other administrators on the campus, each with a particular perspective on the higher education enterprise. Deans must be able to establish credibility, confidence, and effective working relationships among these stakeholders in order to effectively position his or her school and faculty within the campus environment.

Beyond the campus environment, each school is also imbedded within an external inter-organizational network of vested and diverse stakeholders. This network includes, but is not necessarily limited to alumni, the profession, the practice community, prospective employers of graduates, field practicum agencies, grant funders, donors, professional associations, accrediting bodies, etc. Effective transactions with diverse stakeholders involves not only relationship building, but understanding their respective vested interest as it relates to the school and advancing those interests while addressing the needs of the school. Stakeholders at one time or another will see themselves as the primary constituent of the school. While each has legitimate, complementary interests in the school, at times they compete for primacy. The Dean must be able to view the school and these stakeholders from a systems perceptive that allows each to understand the vital role they play in relation to the school while understanding their inter-relationship with each other.

Kotter (1996) stresses the importance of building a common vision among stakeholders within the organization as well as external to it. Vision plays a key role in aligning, directing, and inspiring the actions of a large number of people. "Vision refers to a picture of the future with some implicit or explicit commentary on why people should strive to create that future." (Kotter, 1996, p. 68)

To be effective, a vision must seem reasonable and capture the aspirations and vested interest of stakeholders. Through articulating and building a common vision, Deans, and other administrators can address the interrelatedness of varied interests and better align the interests of diverse stakeholders with the needs of a school. A necessary first step, however, would be that the Dean must have clarity about his or her vision for the school. It may be, for example, that the vision may be to establish a national reputation for the school in the area of research and scholarship. The vision may otherwise be to create a student centered environment and a rigorous, practice-oriented curriculum so the school can be noted for excellence in preparing students for professional practice. In any regard, it is the vision that the Dean helps to lend to the school a move in a certain direction and transcends the day-to-day management functions. It is this vision that helps the Dean transact effectively with the four cultures of the academy and with the internal and external stakeholders. It is, in a word, vision that translates management and administration into leadership.

Training and Degree(s) Required

There are several career paths that can lead to a career as a Social Work Dean or Director. Typically one becomes qualified to be a Dean after establishing him or herself as a senior social work faculty. The position of Dean typically requires that the individual hold the Ph.D. degree as well as either an M.S.W. and/or a B.S.W. Accreditation standards currently require that the Chief Administrative Officer of a social work program either have a CSWE-accredited Master's Social Work degree, with a Doctoral degree preferred, or a professional degree in Social Work from a CSWE-accredited program and a Doctoral degree. The chief administrator also has demonstrated leadership ability through teaching, scholarship, curriculum development, administrative experience, and other academic and professional activities in the field of social work (CSWE, 2001, Accreditation Handbook, p. 38).

The specific desired qualifications for a specific Dean position may vary widely from institution to institution depending on the institution's and program's mission. Larger, "research" institutions typically will seek out individuals that have established themselves in academia as researchers, scholars, and professional leaders. Because of their research mission, the emphasis in such institutions is toward individuals that have demonstrated success and leadership in promoting research and scholarship.

Other institutions with a more comprehensive, "teaching" mission may place less emphasis on accomplished researchers and scholars, but look for individuals with educational and professional leadership experiences. These institutions may look for individuals that can help build strong educational programs and understand curriculum and program development. Still others may look for individuals with either of the above traits coupled with administrative, management experience. The ability to manage personnel, administer a budget, and understand organizational structure and processes become very central to the position of Dean, depending on the size of the program and the complexity of the organizational infrastructure. In smaller programs, the Dean may do it all. In larger programs, other personnel who are available to attend to the day-to-day processes of "running the shop" may support the Dean. In any of the above scenarios, however, it is typically essential that the Dean be someone appropriately established within academia and within the profession.

Personality Traits and Skills Deemed
Important To Succeed

Not too long ago administrators from throughout our university attended a Franklin Covey presentation on the Four Roles of Leadership (Covey, 2003). Covey presents the Four Roles of Leadership as: Modeling, Pathfinding, Aligning, and Empowering. Such a model provides a valuable method to view the tasks associated with providing leadership in Social Work Education.

Pathfinding—Creating the Blueprint: Leadership begins with clarity of thought and purpose. Stephen R. Covey says that all things are created twice—that the "mental creation precedes the physical creation." You wouldn't build a home without a blueprint. Similarly, it's folly to rush into action without understanding your purpose. The Pathfinding role helps create a blueprint of action and ensure that plans have integrity—before one acts.

Aligning—Creating a Technically Elegant System of Work: If Pathfinding identifies a path, aligning paves it. Organizations are aligned to get the results they get. Covey suggests that if you are not getting the results you want, it is due to a misalignment somewhere, and no pushing, pulling, demanding, or insisting will change a misalignment. Therefore, a leader must work to change systems, processes, and structure to align them with the desired results identified through Pathfinding.

Empowering—Releasing the Talent, Energy, and Contribution of People: Covey describes "Empowerment" as an overused term but under-utilized in practice. Empowering isn't abandoning people, letting them "figure it out" on their own. Nor is it allowing individuals minute freedoms while controlling other aspects. True empowerment yields high trust, productive communication between individuals and teams, and innovative results where each member of the team feels welcome to bring his or her genius to the table.

Modeling—Building Trust with Others (The Heart of Effective Leadership):
Covey holds that leadership is not just what a leader does, but who a
leader is. Leadership involves the essential balance between character and
competence. (FranklinCovey, https://cert.franklincovey.com/register/mo
reinfo_4roles.cgi?program_id=8)

Modeling is at the heart of social work. It is the responsibility of faculty, administration, and alumni, to model professional, effective, and ethical practice. Students learn not only in the classroom, but also from every
personal interaction with those working in social work and social work
education.

Pathfinding is a major role of leadership for schools of social work. It
the responsibility of faculty and academic administrators to engage in professional service, research, writing, and other scholarship activities to make
contributions to the body of social work knowledge. Schools increasingly
must be appropriately positioned for leadership within their practice community and within the broader profession.

Aligning is an ongoing and often difficult task. What has made a school
successful in the past will not necessarily be what takes it where it needs to
go in the future. Schools must be adaptive to constantly changing task environments. Contemporarily, schools engage in curriculum revisions designed
to train social workers for effective work in their vision of today's social
work environment.

As with leadership, empowerment is the heart of social work. For academic administrators and faculty, the leadership task is to engage empowering processes with students so they may in turn learn to engage empowering
processes with clients and the special populations they will serve as professionals.

Leadership is not vested only in the Dean. Leadership is in fact a collec-
tively shared trait and responsibility; a leader cannot lead where others will
not follow. It is therefore incumbent upon the leader to be in tune with the
aspirations of the faculty and staff he or she leads. Likewise, faculty and
staff must be willing to follow. Deans, administrators, faculty, staff, alumni,
and students have the privilege and opportunity, and yes, the responsibility,
to provide leadership. Together they each can model, pathfind, align, and
empower the academic unit.

As an administrator, the Dean must understand the importance of leadership and equity as he or she works to balance the interests and needs of
individual faculty and staff units while working collaboratively with the
broader university. It is a Dean's responsibility to, on the one hand, be his

or her unit's strongest advocate, while on the other hand, help faculty and staff respond to institutional priorities.

It is the Dean's responsibility not only to manage well, but also to lead well. The Dean is expected to provide leadership not only to faculty and staff, but across the campus and within the profession and community as well. The Dean's involvement with professional and educational associations beyond the university provides a broader platform from which to understand and address the many issues confronting higher education. Similarly, involvement with professional and community groups can provide an appreciation of the unique role and mission that higher education can play within an increasingly diverse and multicultural society.

The Dean's responsibilities include providing leadership for the university's academic programs, directing educational policy development, strategic academic program planning, academic personnel decisions, and ensuring the quality of academic programs, research, international education, and other units of the university. Successful Deans develop an appreciation of the intricacies of administration in higher education; the importance of participatory collaboration; the need for multi-level communication and transparency; and the need for personal and professional integrity. Given the culture of academia, it is important for the Dean to hold a healthy respect for faculty self-governance, and participatory leadership in guiding educational and administrative decisions. Nonetheless, while the culture values participatory input, it is nonetheless incumbent upon the administrative head to ultimately make decisions, even if at times contrary to faculty wishes. In such instances Deans often strive to keep affected parties informed of the reasoning behind decisions that are made. Most critically, however, the successful academic administrator strives to maintain a high sense of personal and professional integrity.

Edwards and Baskin (1995) in discussing the attributes of "excellent" Deans cite that excellent Deans will:

1. Embody or personify the schools they lead;

2. Establish places for their schools in their universities and communities;

3. Be very effective at developing people and resources;

4. Be able to translate the values of their schools and professions into recognizable, concrete accomplishments—in other words, they "manage for the mission";

5. Have confidence in themselves and their abilities;

6. Inspire hope and optimism that people can grow and develop;

7. Have a strong sense of responsibility for their leadership;

8. Be flexible;

9. Place preeminent value on serving others;

10. Be intensively determined to make their programs work (p 59)

Beyond the competencies of administration and management functions, successful Deans, particularly in social work, tend also to have good "people skills." Management, administration, and leadership involve people processes. Social workers can make good use of their practice skills by applying the interpersonal skills learned in practice in the administrative arena. Interpersonal and use of self, skills learned in casework, group work, and community organization, all are transferable to administration. Ultimately successful leadership in administration builds on good relationship skills and knowledge of human behavior, particularly within an organizational context.

Difficulties of the Work

Even when done well, the job of the Dean is difficult. The demands of administration are multiple and challenging. No day is routine. There are multiple demands for one's time as there is always someone else with whom one has to meet. There are deadlines to meet, reports to write, correspondence that has to be responded to, phone calls to return, etc. Decisions need to be made quickly and with conviction, often with incomplete information. A Dean's time is never his or her own. At time, the most difficult thing to control seems to be the schedule. While the Dean may be the one "in charge," his or her time is often dictated by the need to respond to other people's needs based on their availability.

Thus, positions of leadership and authority, while empowering and fulfilling, are also typically stress filled. The adage, "Uneasy lays the head that wears the throne," applies to most positions of administrative responsibility. As administrator, the Dean is responsible not only for his or her own performance, but for the well being and effective functioning of others within the organization. In a very real sense, the Dean's effectiveness, like most administrators, lies just as much in the performance of others than in his or her personal performance. As the chief administrator, the Dean is responsible for the effective functioning of the academic unit. Others in the organization look to the Dean for leadership, direction, and resources. The Dean must provide needed resource allocation so that others can have the means to fulfill their job responsibilities.

As with any job, the Dean's job also has its share of difficulty. Among the things that make academic life so rich and rewarding is the diversity of perspective evident within the curriculum and among the faculty. Dynamic, strong faculties with diverse perspectives enrich and stimulate the academic experience. They also make it much more difficult to arrive at collective decision-making regarding courses of action that may be needed. The ability to lead is often tested when dealing with strong, dynamic but very differently thinking faculty.

The quality of the work is also a key determinate of job satisfaction and stress for the Dean as well as for others in the organization. When resources are limited, morale will suffer. When morale is low, there tends to be a general drain of energy and dynamism that further contributes to a general malaise. At times like this, it is important to maintain a perspective that allows one to see these dynamics as cyclical and transitory and to focus on the broader aims of the school.

Rewards of the Work

The adage that "a bad day in academia is still better than a good day at _____" attests to the value that one places in the academic life. Regardless of one's role, academe, working at a university, is still among the most fulfilling and rewarding careers available. By its very nature academe is abundant with intrinsic rewards and the ability to affect the future.

The rewards and satisfactions inherent in being a Dean are as varied as the motivations one may have for becoming a Dean. Certainly some are motivated by the status and prestige associated with such a position, others by perceptions of power and authority, others by the rewards of higher salaries associated with the upward mobility afforded by administrative positions. For many the reasons for becoming a Dean are the same reasons they became social workers in the first place: to make a difference, to help mold the direction of social work education and the impact that social work training has on students and the clients they will ultimately serve. For most of us, there comes a point in our careers when we feel we could do something differently if we had the opportunity to be the one in charge. Being a Dean to a faculty member is often akin to the social worker in an agency who decides he or she would do things differently if they were the agency executive. In large measure, we strive to make a difference within the organizations we work with and within the broader profession. The Dean's position provides a ready platform for accomplishing these broader aspirations. The Dean of a school of social work is a position of leadership not only for the school, but for the practice community and profession as well.

How to Get Started on this Career Track

Individuals interested in pursuing a career as a Dean, should first prepare for a career in academia. Working toward a Doctorate either in Social Work or in some other related field with either a Master's or a Bachelor's degree in Social Work would be a necessary first step in that direction. Within their educational training, individuals would be well advised to take coursework in administration and management as well as other macro oriented content such as program development, organizational practice, community practice, policy practice, etc. Master's curricula typically offer these options. Doctoral curricula also provide opportunities for students to develop areas of specialization or cognates. Such cognates can easily accommodate a focus on higher education administration. Throughout their training, whether in macro or direct practice, individuals should be mindful of the transferability of skills and competencies across not only practice settings, but also system levels. Good interpersonal, relationship skills as well as assessment and problem-solving skills are applicable regardless of setting and are essential in administration.

Once in academia, it is important that an individual demonstrate the ability to earn tenure. A Dean will typically be appointed with tenure rights. Generally, a necessary condition for this is that the individual possesses a scholarly or professional record of accomplishment sufficient to warrant awarding of tenure within the institution. Similarly, because the Dean will ultimately review faculty for tenure, it is important that he or she has demonstrated his or her own ability to earn tenure.

A person's academic experiences should also be sufficiently diverse so that the individual develops an understanding of university settings and how they function. This typically should involve participation in the life of the university beyond the social work department. In addition to teaching responsibilities, it is helpful to have administrative experiences, possibly managed or supervised personnel, directed grants, conducted research, and administered projects that have required interdisciplinary work across the university. In addition to community involvement, the individual should also have maintained a high level of involvement in social work education professional organizations such as CSWE, the Society for Social Work Research, the Association of Baccalaureate Program Directors (BPD) and NASW, etc. Through such experiences, individuals gain an appreciation of the role that schools of social work, as well as institutions of higher learning in general can play within a multicultural and diverse setting and they bring to the role of the Dean a fuller experience base from which to approach the position.

References

Bennis, W. and B. Nanus. (1985) Leaders: The Strategies for Taking Charge. New York: Harper and Row Publishers.

Badaracco, J. L. (2002) Leading Quietly: An Unorthodox Guide to Doing the Right Thing. Boston: Harvard Business School Press.

Bennis, W. (1997) Managing People is Like Herding Cats. Provo: Executive Excellence Publishing.

Bennis, W. and B. Nanus (1985) Leaders: The Strategies for Taking Charge. New York: Harper and Row, Publishers.

Berquist, W. H. (1992). The Four Cultures of the Academy: Insights and Strategies for Improving Leadership in Collegiate Organizations (Jossey-Bass)

Council on Social Work Education. (2001). Handbook of Accreditation Standards and Procedures. (Alexandria: CSWE).

Council on Social Work Education (2003). Reporter. (Alexandria: CSWE) Fall.

Covey, S. R. (1989). The 7 Habits of Highly Effective People: Powerful Lessons in Personal Change. New York: Simon & Schuster.

Daniels, A. C. (1994). Bringing Out the Best in People: How to Apply the Astonishing Power of Positive Reinforcement. New York: McGraw-Hill, Inc.

Edwards, R.L. and F. R. Baskin (1995). Providing Leadership. Raymond, F. B., III (ed.) The Administration of Social Work Education Programs: The Roles of Deans and Directors. National Association of Deans and Directors of Schools of Social Work.

Franklin Covey (2003). The 4 Roles of Leadership® Workshop. Arlington, TX.

Franklin Covey (2004) Website. https://cert.franklincovey.com/register/moreinfo_4roles.cgi?program_id=8)

Hackman, M. Z. and C. E. Johnson (1991). Leadership: a Communication Perspective. Prospect Heights: Waveland Press, Inc.

Kottner, J. P. (1996). Leading Change. Boston: Harvard Business School Press.

McCauley, C. D, Moxley, R. S., and E. Van Velsor. (1998). Handbook of Leadership Development. San Francisco: Jossey-Bass

Raymond, F. B., III (ed.) (1995). The Administration of Social Work Education Programs: The Roles of Deans and Directors. National Association of Deans and Directors of Schools of Social Work.

Weinbach, R. W. (1994). The Social Worker as Manager (2nd Edition). Boston: Allyn and Bacon.

6

A Peek Behind the Scenes with a Domestic Violence Shelter Director

ℰℭ

Kim Denton

Nature of the Work

There are times that I sit at my desk and gaze out the window. As I look at the world outside that window I see how innocent and peaceful it appears. But at the same time my mind seems to battle with anger that my job is even necessary. I am the director of a domestic violence shelter. I feel that it is unfortunate that a shelter even has to exist, but at some point in our society, violence against an intimate partner was not approved but rather accepted.

I can't say that I dislike my job; that is not it at all. I find great pleasure helping victims of domestic violence reclaim their lives. Many victims have entered these shelter doors thinking that they were worthless and guilty of provoking the trauma in their life. Of those victims many of them have exited the shelter with a renewed sense of spirit and a feeling of self-worth. Those are the victims that validate my reasons for being here; they are the victims that give shelter advocates the stamina to continuing fighting for them.

There are many rewards in that. If you can imagine for a minute that life around you has come to the point of total chaos. You have spiritually, emotionally, and physically reached the point where you are lost. If you turn one way, does it guide you home to safety? What is safety? What is home? Home for victims of domestic violence has become something different than they were used to growing up. That is, if they grew up in a family like the Cleaver's, where life was roses. Then one day they find themselves all of a sudden stuck in a family like the Menendez brothers, where on the surface family life looked like the Cleaver's, but in the scheme of things life was full of manipulation, control, and abuse. The change takes time so therefore isn't as noticeable to the victim, but one day they realize the difference and have no idea what to do.

I discovered long ago that working in a helping profession would not make me rich. I also discovered that helping someone turn his or her life around is priceless. No amount of money in the world could equal the satisfaction that comes from watching a beaten woman evolve into a healthy human being.

In the scope of things fighting against this crime takes a lot of dedication. In another world family life would be like a vase of fresh flowers that never wilt. We don't live in that world. In this world violence exists in homes on every block. Children hide in closets or under tables as they witness their parents withstand blows to their head. Some sit through school wondering if their mother or father will be alive when they get home. Some of them never breathe a word of their secret life; others communicate it in ways of negative behavior. They turn to drugs to dull the pain, they find control in their life through eating disorders, and they learn to believe that this kind of life is normal, so they, in turn, live a life of abuse, becoming violent criminals or commit suicide. Others walk in misery and guilt forever.

Through all of that I'm sure you can see that the nature of this work is unpredictable. There is no such thing as "an average day." There are days when the sounds behind the walls are quiet and the phones are silent, and then there are other days when the sounds behind the walls are loud and the phones are ringing constantly. I have learned to cherish the quiet days and use them as a time to catch my breath because it is very possible that the next minute could signal a cry of help or assistance and the rest of the day or week will be hectic.

Training and Degrees Required

Domestic violence is very difficult to understand and because of this, training is an ongoing task. Workers in the field of domestic violence have a variety of college degrees such as criminology, social work, or human services. An awareness of mental health is also a benefit. No particular training or degree will completely prepare anyone for the job. Personally, I felt Not-for-Profit Management, Interviewing Techniques, Social Problems, Family Violence, Practical Human Services, Psychology, Law and Ethics, and State and Local Government were helpful courses. There are many others.

I find that many victims of domestic violence or child abuse have the desire to enter this field, which is wonderful; they have the ability to relate to the victim on a different level than a person who has never experienced abuse. However, if that person has not reached a complete level of healing, then wounds reopen and make life difficult. We have one board member who is a survivor of domestic violence. She has been out of the situation for many years, but still cannot find the strength to answer the crisis hotline. Only the survivor can know when they are ready to help others heal, but they must be very honest with themselves before considering it.

Personality Traits and Skills Deemed
Important to Succeed

As the director of the shelter all of the responsibilities are on my shoulders. I manage the budget, staff, and programs, and make the final decisions. My thoughts must constantly be observing and overseeing. I am fortunate that my staff is very efficient and often times do not need my supervision. If they need guidance I trust that they will come to me. But at the same time, their actions represent the shelter and ultimately are my responsibility.

My shoulders may carry some heavy weight, but I still have it made. I work forty hours a week (some are more some are less) sitting behind a desk. In the summer's heat I am in the cool air conditioning and in the dead of winter I am sitting nice and cozy at my desk. For the most part I can come and go when I want and the only people I answer to are the board of directors. Sounds like the ideal job, right? Well, okay, it has some perks, but one must be wise not to let all that go to their head.

In my opinion any good leader or manager is willing to roll up their sleeves and also get their hands dirty. I would never dream of asking my staff to do something that I would not be willing to do myself. As I have said before my staff is efficient, but that is an understatement. They are remarkable and a blessing from God. Sometimes what they encounter on the front lines is shattering.

One day an advocate went with a client to court. It was a typical child custody hearing; we didn't expect this one to be any different then any other hearing. But it was different. This client's abuser was armed with enough ammunition to be awarded custody of the children. Apparently the client had been withholding some very powerful information from her attorney and from the advocates. She thought "out of sight, out of mind." But her husband brought it to sight and used it to his advantage to win. Like any other mother who loves her children, the client was devastated. Within hours she would have to hand her children over to a man who had been emotionally abusive and there was nothing she could do about it.

For the advocate it was shock. This was her first court case. I and another advocate had trained her before and told her what to expect. We thought we had all the pieces together, but we didn't know about the hidden secret that held so much power. When they returned I had two traumas to deal with, a devastated mother and a dazed advocate. Clearly the advocate had done nothing wrong, but she felt the impact and witnessed the client's world being destroyed.

I tell the advocates that they are like the coach of an athletic team. They train and prepare the team for victory. When the team loses the advocates are there, when the team wins the advocate is there. Unlike the coach of that athletic team, the advocates name is never mentioned. Well sometimes it is, but it shouldn't be if at all possible. You see, the batterer looks at the advocate as the reason the victim can't be controlled anymore. It is her fault that the victim won't return to the home. Once that control is lost the batterer will grab another tactic. Domestic violence is about control. There are many tactics that are used, and when one doesn't work anymore, another with more heat is chosen; for the advocate that can mean danger.

Let me give you another story. Less than a year ago, one of the advocates was in a video store with her family. Inside the store was a past client's son who had stayed at the shelter for some period of time. This child happened to be with his father, AKA the batterer, for weekend visitation (yes, even batterers have a right to visitation or at least that is the opinion of some officials). This child informed his father of the advocate and essentially made her a sitting duck.

Right there in the video store this man approached her. He came very close to her, looked her in the eye, and in a loud gruff voice said, "I do not abuse my wife." I'm sure that if you asked the advocate she would tell you that she was intimidated that day. And if she was honest she would also say her salary wasn't worth it.

Safety issues are always on the forefront of our minds. Advocates can protect themselves by only using their first names and they eliminate all personal identifiers from their conversations. As director, my name is everywhere. If I give a press release there is a quote, "Denton said..." If I take a picture for the media there is my name and face plastered for all to see. (This is very humbling I might add.) I have found that just going to Wal-Mart is not a personal endeavor anymore. We're a small community so people get to know each other. They see me and they associate me with the shelter. They may not remember my name, but they know what I represent. That can be rather challenging when one of my children are misbehaving in public.

This position is not cut and dry, not black and white, therefore many skills are helpful. One of the most important skills is the ability to operate finances. Our budget is in the area of $300,000, which is one of the lowest in the state of Indiana. There are many revenue sources for this money. The tricky part is those revenue sources determine what expenses they will pay and which ones they won't. This must be very carefully monitored to be sure the wrong expenses are not paid with the funder's money, otherwise there is the risk of refunding it and/or losing it all together. This requires attention to detail and organization. Let me explain further.

A large portion of our funding comes from the Indiana Family and Social Services Administration. We receive five different grants from them and about 52 percent of our revenue. As mentioned above each grant has different specifics, but yet they are close enough in some areas that they can pay the same expenses. A lot of detail and organization comes into play with this because all of that has to be kept separate and there must be a reason for every expense allocation made with their money. For example, if a portion of someone's salary is paid with a grant there must be a clear definition why that portion was applied to his or her salary. Or if a portion of the utility bill was paid, how was that portion determined and how did the amount get connected to that particular revenue source.

Business skills overall are very important. Our agency, like many other social agencies, is considered not-for-profit. This clearly means that we cannot make any money. If we do then we must find a way to spend it. Not necessarily a bad problem, but one that is not very often faced. There are always shortages in the budget and always new projects that can be created, but managing the finances on a shoestring budget while still being efficient in meeting the needs of domestic violence victims, requires a lot of strategy.

A very good skill to have on hand is knowledge in grant writing. There is never enough money and there is always a new program that would help achieve the mission. Recognizing that a new program would help is one thing, getting it started and running is another. Why? The bottom line of the budget is always in the red, where will money for a new program come from? It doesn't fall from the sky and thus keeps the agency from growing. But it would help achieve the mission! I know, so therefore searching for grant money is continuous. Once a potential funder is found the grant must be written under the guidelines stated. Some grants are easy to write, others are more difficult. Regardless a lot of time is absorbed searching, writing, and then if received, reporting.

I have found that marketing and public relations is also important, especially for the benefit of the victim, but also for public awareness and support. Raising money is always easier when the community knows who we are and why we exist. People are more likely to be supportive then. Sometimes I will ask people, "If you ask a stranger for a favor what will they say? If you ask your friend for a favor what will they say?" It is more likely that the friend will help you and less likely that the stranger will help you. So in the not-for-profit world it is good to have a lot of friends. Marketing is only one way to get the word out; public relations is another. When fighting against domestic violence, there is going to be obstacles that the victim will have to overcome. When the agency has a strong relationship with the community, then it is easier to overcome those obstacles.

Thus another important feature of operating a domestic violence shelter is coordinating with other social agencies. Each of them offers direct services to the client, but no one offers enough services across the board to be a one-stop shop for the victim. Therefore all agencies come together as one. For instance, WorkOne will assist with employment, Welfare will assist with finances, Step Ahead helps with day care, and us with housing. Through everyone working together the end result is the same.

For example, recently a victim entered the shelter after an altercation with her boyfriend. The altercation was somewhat severe to the point of restraining her from leaving the home. When she did find a chance to leave the only thing on her mind was finding safety, which she accomplished, but in doing so she left behind her prescriptions. Replacing prescriptions can be difficult, but with help from our friends, AKA a local agency, we were able to get her meds refilled without much problem. However, without a collaborative relationship this would not have gone as smoothly.

Managing employees is yet one more skill that is important. They are vital to the agency and invaluable. Every Christmas, I struggle with what to give them because no amount of money or gift is enough. Without them I could not make this agency successful, but more importantly without them we could not make a difference in the world. At the same time they are working in a not-for-profit world where salaries are not going to make it possible for them to drive fancy cars or live in luxury homes. Their biggest reward is witnessing a victim transform his or her life. While that may seem like enough sometimes we find ourselves questioning.

Difficulties of the Work

Victims of domestic violence go through a horrendous amount of manipulation and control tactics. To someone who has not been in that type of situation it all seems so easy, "Just leave." But it isn't easy. Batterers do not show characteristics of control in the beginning of the relationship and if they were to hit their victim right from the start the victim would be wise enough to leave because mentally he or she hasn't been broken down yet. Instead, in the beginning, the batterer uses tactics that are more subconscious that will gradually tear down the victim to a state where their emotional strength is destroyed. So then when the lies and the manipulation come back, either in an effort to keep control or regain control, it becomes emotionally difficult and hard to make a rational decision.

For the victim's advocate the decision is clear. But the advocate understands the manipulation and the lies and some can even verbalize what the batterer said or will say without the victim ever verbalizing it. The role of the advocate is to educate, support, and advocate. An analogy we use is we plant seeds, the victim chooses what to do with that seed. He or she may nourish it and it may grow or she may leave it dormant. If dormant is her choice, then the seed will lie there until she decides to nourish it.

Rewards of the Work

Watching the victim nourish it is the rewards of the work. When I first came to work at the shelter I was an advocate. My very first client was a middle-aged woman and two children. Her history of abuse was a nightmare. As a new employee who didn't completely understand all the dynamics of abuse, I was overwhelmed. I literally did not know what to do with this woman. Lucky for me she already had a seed planted and she knew where she was going. By the time I came in she was nourishing her seed. This woman was an inspiration. She was a full-time college student, not to mention a full-time mother. She would sit up late at night studying, then turn around and be up first thing the next morning to get to the kids off to school and get herself off to college.

A normal length of stay at the shelter is 30-45 days. Her stay was extended due to problems securing housing. After all, what landlord is willing to rent to an abused woman with no job? At the time, government housing assistance was frozen and government subsidized housing in our community was full with a long waiting list. Neither routes were an option for her; we had hit a brick wall. The only thing left to do was to wait. Finally an apartment came through and she was on her way.

She made the next stage and was able to progress her situation, but that is only the tip of the iceberg. About two years ago the assistant director and I received an invitation in the mail for her college graduation. This woman did not only graduate with a Bachelor's degree, but she was also magna cum laude. A year later she bought her first home. Today she is working and living a life free of violence. Her story is a fine example of how the seed becomes nourished and how it can bear fruit. Watching her gave me hope.

Unfortunately not all stories are this wonderful. The flip side of that are many victims of domestic violence return to the abuser. Actually statistics tell us that they leave seven to eight times before leaving for good. Because of that the emotional side of working in domestic violence can be difficult. Sometimes I wonder if we really are making a difference. It is like a roller coaster. You fight like crazy to get through the obstacles for a little piece of heaven, and then catch your breath so you can do it all over again. All the while understanding that the victim is the one at the controls, not you. You can't make decisions for her; all you can do is lay her options on the table and support her when she chooses. If she chooses to return to the home it can be very difficult because you know life free of violence is possible and you know how to go about getting it, but that isn't a package that you can hand over.

The burnout rate in this field is very high. I have watched new employees come into the shelter thinking they are going to, "help people." Then they discover that the reality is people have to want help first. That it isn't as glorious as they had thought. They discover that the world has valleys of darkness and sometimes that valley can be overwhelming.

My goal as director is to screen new employees for that unrealistic view of the world. I want staff members who will understand they are not in control; the victim is in control. But in order to help her they will have to go to her world. The trick is being able to pull yourself back out of her world when the shift is over, better known as the ability to have empathy. In a way it is just like all the cartoons, where the characters are able to do some kind of swipe into another time period or another world and then swipe right back to their real life.

How to Get Started on This Career Track

There is no secret code to getting started in this line of work; one can begin by simply applying at a shelter and working within the program. Large shelters have many facets of their program such as legal advocates, case managers, child advocates, outreach advocates, house managers, and program directors. For the most part anyone entering this field must understand that every single client has a different story. No one case will ever be the same as another. They must also realize that the product we are providing is a service to people. That alone indicates nothing will ever be customary.

As I said before there are perks to my job, but there is also stress and burnout. Some days I feel like a fish in a blender and it must show on my face because even my dog has come to understand when I am stressed. Hearing stories can break your heart, seeing the children come and go is difficult, pressure of a grant deadline can be frazzling, realizing my co-workers are at risk terrifies me, watching a victim walk back into a war zone can make us feel like failures, and making unfavorable decisions is not easy. But stress is what I decide it is and only it can control as much of my life that I allow it to. So I find a way to manage it.

There are times when I ask God if this is a temporary assignment. There are other times when I beg him to make it temporary. But when I sit at my desk and look out the window, I see the green grass, the blue sky, I hear the children playing, I also see the images of the Cleaver's, and the vase of flowers that will never wilt, and I remember the smiles of survivors. I hold on to their success stories and I cherish them. It is those stories that remind me that it is possible to overcome the violence. I tell myself that their success is not mine and their failure is not mine, they only allowed me to walk with them. In the end the journey will be priceless.

7

GERIATRICS SOCIAL WORK

℘ℭℜ

Tina Vickery

Nature of the Work

There are various employment opportunities for those who have the desire to work with the geriatric population. The amount of direct client services you are interested in providing will impact your decision on the career choices you make.

Agencies including The Division of Aging and local community service centers employ social workers that have training or experience working with the geriatric population. The amount of direct client service that is provided by the social worker depends on the nature of the position. Case managers have more direct contact with the client than an individual holding a supervisory position.

Another area of employment that offers the social worker the opportunity to provide both direct and indirect services are in long-term care facilities.

This chapter will deal with social work in long-term care facilities due to the wide variety of skills required of the social worker in this position. Long-term care facilities are federally mandated to provide sufficient and appropriate social services to their residents. The facility must identify the need for medically related social services for each individual. Medically related social services means services to assist the patient in maintaining or improving their ability to manage their every day physical, mental, and psychosocial needs.

As a social worker in long-term care facilities you will become part of an interdisciplinary team, which includes nursing, dietary, therapies, and activities.

The residents' physical and emotional needs are assessed and each member of the team will address their areas of expertise in a written plan of care. Social work in long-term care can be extremely enlightening and often a major educational experience.

Training and Degrees Required

The level of training and type of degree required in the field of gerontology vary among agencies and establishments. Most agencies that specialize in geriatric services require a minimum of a Bachelor's degree in social work or a related field. Position of supervisory nature or within specialized establishments, such as geriatric behavioral centers, require an individual with a Master's degree.

The federal government regulates employment requirements in long-term care facilities. Facilities that have 120 beds or more must hire an individual with a minimum of a Bachelor's degree in a human service field including, but not limited to psychology, special education, rehabilitation counseling, sociology, or social work.

Smaller facilities, especially those located in rural areas, may hire an individual that has taken a specialized course in long-term care social services, which is approved by the states' Department of Health. A company that provides social service consultation services usually teaches the course. Individuals who successfully complete the course are given a certificate allowing them to work as a social service assistant in large facilities or as a social service director in small facilities, under the direction of a visiting consultant specializing in long-term care social services.

I would highly recommend anyone interested in working in long-term care take the course provided by your state. It is not mandatory to be employed in a long-term care facility to enroll. The course is held approximately two times a year. It consists of eight-hour days lasting for the duration of two to three weeks depending upon your state.

Personality Traits Deemed Important
to Succeed

It is the desire to help others and have a caring nature that is probably the most important personality trait required to be a social service worker in any field. An individual must have a genuine concern for the elderly to be successful in the field of gerontology.

The duties and responsibilities of the social worker employed in long-term care can be numerous and the case load extremely high, therefore another important trait is that of good organizational skills. The social worker must be able to productively utilize the time they have. Spending needless time searching for forms and reports will ultimately set you behind, not to mention add needless stress.

The ability to prioritize is another necessary trait. I would suggest you keep a notepad in your pocket to log the tasks you need to perform, and as new ones arise, add them to the list in accordance to their importance. It is not uncommon for numerous tasks to arise during the course of your day. Many times you are approached with issues as you are working on another. Unless you have an extraordinary memory, it is very easy to overlook items that could later cause you much trouble.

The ability to communicate well with others is imperative. As the social worker in a long-term care facility you must not only be capable of communicating well with the residents, but you must be able to communicate with the families of these residents, other staff members, supervisors, outside agencies, physicians, and in some instances lawyers and judges. You will also be responsible for educating staff members about resident rights, behavioral management, and abuse and neglect. Being able to communicate is a necessity.

The last trait I will address is the ability to assess your own emotions and stress level. Being the person that everyone depends upon to solve issues on a daily basis can become taxing at times. A good social worker is able to recognize the signs of burnout and address them before they get out of hand. Take time for yourself. One of the traps social workers in long-term care fall into is working through their lunch and breaks. They become absorbed by the work or time schedules and often either fail to take their lunch break or spend it at their desk eating junk food while finishing paperwork. Ultimately this will catch up with you. Addressing your own needs is an essential necessity.

Difficulties of the Work

As with any field of work the social worker chooses to pursue, there are always some form of difficulties. One very important bit of advice I give to anyone seeking employment in long-term care is to throw out the misconception that nursing homes or long-term care facilities are a place of peace and serenity. Nothing could be further from the truth. One of the biggest difficulties in long-term care is the inability to ever plan your agenda. Try as you might you will never find a day when you can plan your task and keep them in the order you would like to accomplish them. Duties are numerous and often more are added to your day than you anticipated. The social worker in long-term care provides a number of services including, but not limited to the following:

1. Assisting the patient to determine how they would like to make decisions to their health care and whether or not they wish someone else to be involved.

2. Assisting in financial and legal matters.

3. Educating staff on how to support and understand the patients' needs.

4. Assisting patients to obtain needed services, including eye, dental, and audiologist exams.

5. Assisting patients to obtain clothing and personal items.

6. Assisting the patient to obtain services from outside agencies such as wheelchair transportation and absentee voting.

7. Providing any needed counseling services.

8. Constructing individual discharge plans.

9. Educating staff on patient behaviors, why they occur, and interventions.

10. Being a member on committees such as nutritional at risk, incidents and accidents, and behavioral management.

11. Constructing individualized care plans.

12. Contributing your area of expertise to the required MDS assessment.

13. Conducting admission psychosocial/social history assessments.

14. Performing cognitive and depression screening with each patient.

15. Providing one-on-one socialization and counseling to patients.

16. Conducting or participating in resident council meetings.

17. Providing family education on dementia and Alzheimer's disease.

These are only a few of the responsibilities of the social worker in long-term care facilities. There will be times when an unexpected crisis arises pulling the social worker away from these duties. Therefore, as previously mentioned in this chapter, it is essential to have good organizational skills. Tasks can never be pushed aside for the last minute because one never knows what the last minute has in store for them.

Another difficulty in long-term care is the increased admissions of patients who are not in the standard geriatric age group. It is not uncommon to have patients who are in the age group of mid-twenties to fifty years of age. Many of these patients are mentally and or physically handicapped. Therefore it is essential for the social worker to have the educational knowledge or training to be able to service these patients' needs. These patients will need services and support that often differs greatly from the geriatric patient.

The rise in admission of geriatric patients with mental illnesses has also risen in the past decade. Unfortunately, there are very few establishments that specialize in long-term care for the geriatric mentally ill. Many establishments provide short-term treatment designed to regulate patients' medications and provide short-term relief of acute episodes. Establishments that are designed to provide long-term care to these patients are very often full or are in inconvenient locations for family members. A solid knowledge of psychopathology is important. The social worker ultimately utilizes much of their time caring for the mentally ill patient due to behaviors that must be monitored closely. It is important to be able to recognize triggers that may precipitate or cause behaviors to occur.

Another difficulty of the work is becoming too emotionally involved with the patients/residents. The social worker in a long-term care facility has daily contact with the residents and often times their family members. If you calcu-late the waking time spent with the residents it often amounts to more waking time than you spend with your own family. It is virtually impossible not to get emotionally attached to the residents. It is not uncommon to work with a patient for five or more years. Unfortunately patients who are admitted as long-term placements are eventually going to decline cognitively and physi-cally. Death is a natural process and occurs on a regular basis in long-term care facilities. The social worker must be able to deal with his or her own grief during this process and be able to support the resident, their family, and the friends the resident has made during their stay.

Rewards of the Work

Now that you have read all of the difficulties, you are probably asking, "Why on earth would anyone want to pursue a career in long-term care?" Well the answer is simple. If you have been privileged to spend time with a grandparent and experienced the deep affection they have for others or lis-tened to the vast amount of knowledge they have gained during their life, you can easily understand. The emotional reward you experience when you have made someone else's life more comforting is a profound feeling. To be able to ensure that the elderly patient sustains their individual rights and dignity as a human being is gratifying. The social worker in long-term care has the opportunity to meet a vast array of people and professionals in many fields. These contacts can ultimately become a network of opportunities for you in the future, not to mention the numerous friendships you have gained in the process. Regardless of the career path you choose, the fact that you are will-ing to help others and make positive changes is a reward in itself.

How to Get Started on This Career Track

Volunteer work is a positive step toward getting your foot in the door. Often establishments do not advertise position openings simply because they retain a file with submitted resumes. I would recommend sending your re-sume to several establishments, expressing your desire to obtain employment. It is a good idea to mention you would be willing to accept an alternative position such as a social service assistant or an activity coordinator to gain knowledge and experience in the field.

Another avenue to pursue is contacting a long-term care recruiter. Many facilities utilize a recruiter to help fill social service positions. The recruiter keeps a list of professionals and their job preferences. When positions become available they contact the applicant to inform them of the opening. If the applicant is interested the recruiter arranges an interview and acts as a mediator to iron out details.

You can also seek information by contacting a social service consulting firm. You can obtain contact names and numbers by calling either your State Department of Health or any long-term care facility.

8

SOCIAL WORK CAREER PATH AS A GROUP FACILITATOR

ಬಂಡಿ

Rosemary Bell

Nature of the Work

One of the very important mental health intervention resources for social workers is the use of group work. This work is done in what is called the "group format" to provide intervention dynamics that are not available or not practical in individual counseling sessions. It is critically important that the professional who is leading the group be strong in both their understanding of multiple theories of human behavior and in their own communication expertise. The group leader may be identified as a counselor, a therapist, or as a facilitator. In addition, I suggest that the skilled group leader's objectives are to function as an orchestrator of the group in such a manner as to heighten the benefit for each member *and* for the group as a whole. In doing so, the leader is working with a number of individual clients who come together as a unit. However, all group work is about the whole unit, the *group* itself, rather than meeting the needs of one specific individual. The group leader has the responsibility to provide the safest arena for each member of the group, enhancing his or her own growth opportunity, while protecting the cohesiveness of the group as a unit. It is this dual role, this "ying and yang" position of the group leader that makes group work one of the most challenging and rewarding professions in social work.

Training and Degrees Required

In the mental health/therapeutic field it is critically important to have a solid educational background. The social work undergraduate class work and internship opportunities are important avenues that can lead to a career in the field of group work interventions. Course work is available that dissects the multiple facets of group therapy interventions and group dynamics. Of the many theories of human behavior, from which a social worker may draw, the majority lend themselves to use in group work. It is in studying the phenomenon of group *dynamics* that we begin to gain insight into the critical role of the group leader. Most of the theories are easy enough to comprehend. The goal is to help clients gain their own understanding of human behavior and how a particular concept is to some degree their prescription for good mental health. It is the group *dynamics* that require sharpness of skills from a group leader as he or she enables a group of clients, working as a unit and independently at varying rates of healing/learning/growing, which make and sustain group work as continually challenging and absorbing to the social worker.

The opportunity to learn from experience begins once the social work student begins his or her own work as an intern in a social services setting. Ultimately, experience is the most critical teacher for the student anticipating a career specializing in group work. This experiential learning continues throughout the social worker's professional life. I attribute the ongoing learning experience to what is known as the human condition. Each time the social worker comes together with a new group of clients, he or she comes together with a new set of *group dynamics* never before encountered. Each group has its own unique way of responding and reacting to each other, to the curriculum or purpose, and to the group leader.

Almost all social services agencies require their staff members to have a minimum of an undergraduate degree to serve as group leader (counselor, therapist, or facilitator). During internships, the undergraduate student is generally placed alongside a staff member with minimum of a BSW as assistant group leader. The requirement for credentials varies among social service agencies. The type of group is also a factor that determines if the group leader must be a social worker licensed by the state and the level of licensure required. An example might be a psychiatric hospital setting. An intern along with a BSW staff can lead groups that are non-therapeutic. Groups that are therapeutic will require an advanced degree, an MSW. When third party payment is an issue, there will be a requirement for state licensure and prior approval by the third party payee.

Types of Groups

All group work is not the same. The purpose and the function of the group work can be identified in three major areas depending on identified objectives. The three types of groups are (1) support groups (2) educational groups and (3) therapy groups. However, the identity of the group does not prohibit any one of these benefits possibly occurring for the client's benefit. Example: the therapeutic group will include education and the educational group will include support. The support group might have moments of real therapeutic intervention. It is only limited by the skills of the leader.

Support Groups are a means for individuals with similar challenges to come together and provide help and encouragement to each other. The group leader functions primarily as a facilitator who oversees the group to increase equality and appropriateness among the members. The facilitator may or may not provide feedback to what is shared by group members. In the support group it is wise to establish guidelines sometimes called "group norms." This information is often posted on the wall to set healthy guidelines on which each group member can rely and to which they may be held accountable. Most support groups do *not* require that the members participate verbally other than acknowledging their name and how they have a commonality with the other group members. The support group is sometimes called a "process group" where group members can process with caring people their challenges, their brokenness, and their successes. Group size may range from three to twelve members. The group facilitator does not provide topic or curriculum. This is determined by the needs of the group. Attendance on a specific schedule is not mandatory. Commitment to **confidentiality** is mandatory.

Educational Groups allow the social worker an opportunity to provide meaningful information in a teaching format to a group of clients. Social service agencies generally have specific outreach functions. Providing useful information to a group of clients adds to the agency's efficiency. Educational information includes such subjects as alcohol and drug use facts, understanding your mental illness, anger management skills, or positive self-esteem (and many other topics). The group provides a useful teaching format by combining the knowledge and expertise of the group leader and adds the benefit of what group members can contribute out of their own experience. Group size can range from three to fifteen members. Educational groups are generally for a specific number of sessions in order to cover the designated material effectively. Group members are generally required to make a commitment to attendance. Commitment to *confidentiality* is mandatory.

Therapeutic Groups are less common. The therapeutic group's primary function is to provide a safe environment in which to openly share with others the issues surrounding some painful and traumatic event from the past. The identified goal of the therapeutic group work is healing emotional/psychological damage. The mental health population that utilizes this type of group work might be agencies dealing with PTSD, family violence, grief and loss counseling, childhood abuse issues, victims of violent crimes, etc. Therapeutic groups require highly skilled leaders with a minimum of an MSW. Therapy groups generally limit membership to six and can be as small as two members. Commitment to **confidentiality** is mandatory.

Personality Traits and Skills Deemed
Important to Succeed

What determines which social worker might work effectively as a group leader *and* find it rewarding? I think the group leader must first of all be very healthy themselves by having tended to all their own psychological and emotional issues. In the group setting *all* possible issues come to the surface. The demonstration of healthy personal boundaries by the group leader is to model appropriate behavior to the client. The leader will only be effective as long as he or she remains totally objective.

Another important trait of the leader is their ability to take in and retain multiple facts about the group members as individuals in order to maximize any opportunity to address or relate what another member says to them. Example: two sessions prior, group member "x" mentioned having been compromised by something specific. This session group member "y" shares that she was just compromised (whatever) by a similar circumstance. After "y" shares appropriately, the group leader will call "x" by name and ask "and wasn't that similar to what you were sharing two weeks ago?" What might follow then are the two group members identifying their shared experience in a mutually beneficial way. This type of situation is what brings real cohesiveness to the group.

A third important facet to a good group leader's personality is the ability to always exhibit a demeanor that he or she is in charge, yet never be controlling. I believe this will be demonstrated more by demeanor than by overt actions or statements. The group will pick up on their leader's self-confidence and personal strength. The group leader's ability to communicate being "in-charge" of their self creates a sense of safety to members and increases their confidence in the group process.

A balanced sense of humor is another group-leader strength. It is important that time spent in the group is not all just hard work. The levity gained from an appropriate, funny anecdote or cartoon is beneficial to the group member's enjoyment and to their being truly comfortable. Everyone who cries together also does better if they occasionally laugh together.

A critically important personality trait for the group leader is the ability to remain non-judgmental. This is, of course, a primary part of our social work ethics. In the group setting where many stories and experiences are shared, the leader will hear of behavioral choices from clients that have been destructive to self and others. Remaining non-judgmental and accepting the person apart from their behaviors is a critical link to encouraging new growth and change. Remember that facial expressions can reveal what words will not say. Group leaders must monitor their own facial expressions and body language at the same time they are observing these aspects of the client. In the event of negative disclosure by group members a good leader will always manage to keep his or her facial expression in neutral. However, in the event of positive disclosure and successes, it is important that the leader openly express approval and support of the client.

Difficulties of the Work

So what is it that makes leading groups challenging? In my experience leading a group is not more difficult than doing individual sessions. It is just different. The demands vary. Some objectives are different. But both types of mental health work are challenging, sometimes hard, and always require the social worker to exhibit well-honed skills and extraordinary insightfulness about human behavior. However, in group work the leader does become somewhat the person on the "conductor's platform." To skillfully orchestrate the healthiest outcome for the most clients **is** what continually challenges the group leader. To bring forth the most productive contributions and to lessen the more destructive offerings, or to reframe the destructive contributions into something positive and beneficial to the entire group, requires an expertise and ability more than textbook knowledge, it requires knowledge, plus skills, plus experience.

What I determine to be additionally difficult about the role of the group leader is the random mix of clients. Here are some particularly challenging client types that the leader will encounter.

In almost every group there will be one client who wants to be the co-leader or *co-therapist*. This is predictable in all types of groups. Generally this client has been in some type of mental health counseling long enough to know descriptive words and terms for many mental health issues/diagnosis. Often they have read "too many" self-help books and applied too little information to themselves. They are quick to diagnose other client's issues and offer them advice. This client will identify themselves early and the leader must privately help the client understand that their role is limited to group member only.

Another typical group member is the *attention seeker*. This client will speak out too frequently and attempt to make his or her story just a little more severe than anyone else's situation. Again, the leader might address this "interrupting" factor privately or very tactfully address it in the group to identify emotional needs that drive this type of behavior.

Every group has at least one member who tries to be *invisible*. This client sits back in a timid position and avoids eye contact. There is little affect demonstrated. The group leader seeks to increase this client's comfort level with pleasant but quick glances. In time, there will be evidence (small changes in facial expression) that indicates the client is becoming more engaged in the group process. The leader's best tactic would then be to call the client by name and ask a question requiring just a one-word response. An example might be, "Do you relate to what was just said, Mary?" This will gently bring the "invisible" client into better group focus. In time this client may contribute meaningfully to the group process.

The *reluctant* client is the one in the group who just does not believe they should have to be there. This individual may have joined the group due to some outside leverage such as a court order. This may be from a criminal court or a civil court. This person's resistance is typically because they are still in denial about their mental health issues and their need for change. The client may be court mandated or they may be "family" mandated. The have come to group only due to an outside force, not because they want to do the hard work of changing unhealthy thinking and self-defeating behavioral patterns. In a well led and purpose focused group this client generally responds favorably after a few sessions. If not, and their reluctant attitude becomes negative for the group, then the group leader will privately confront the client and identify the conditions under which he or she can remain in the group.

One characteristic that can increase the challenges for the leader is the client's tendency to compare histories and experiences. It is detrimental to a client's progress if they discount their own pain because they hear how another's journey has been more chaotic and damaging. Clients will often need to be reminded that this type of comparison is a form of self-discounting and will limit their progress to an even better psychological place. Part of the leader's challenge is to keep each client focused on his or her own needs as they make contributions from their own experience that will in some way benefit other group members. If at any time a group member attempts to discount someone else's experience by pointing out their greater suffering, the group leader must address that inappropriate behavior directly. The responsibility to keep all clients responsible to both self and to the other group members is quite a challenge.

Rewards of the Work

So you want to know how all these challenges can be worth it? I think your working toward a degree in social work already tells me a lot about you. Only students who desire to bring positive change to social systems, to communities, and to individuals are in these classes. The fact that you care about people will be a primary reward. It is amazing to see results from the fact that I care about a client's quality of life. The client may begin to care. Or they may begin to care a little bit. It is that "little bit" of change in how the client interprets their worth and value that becomes the turning point of the change process. To be able to impact another person's positive growth and development can be a major reinforcement to your own sense of purpose. The contribution is immeasurable. So much of the pain and suffering in our society is due to generational dysfunction. Each time an individual becomes emotionally and psychologically healthier, they become contributors to a healthier next generation. The reward for the group leader is the knowledge that at least you have planted a good seed. The occasions when you do see lives turned around from despair to hope, the reward is your own gratitude to have been a part of another's journey. I think that is what social work is all about.

How to Get Started on This Career Track

Many factors enter the picture when attempting to find the job you most want. But why not start there? Know what population you most want to work with. Know the details. Identify the establishment or agencies most likely to concentrate on that population. If you plan to specialize in working with adolescents, for example, start out where you most believe you want to be. Utilize networking opportunities through whatever resources you may have. Seek information through your state social work association or our NASW. Be willing to make sacrifices such as moving to where a job is available. When possible, seek an internship that will allow you to get experience doing group work. The best situation is often to have the good fortune to be hired by the same agency. Getting experience and good references will be important to achieving your career goals. If jobs are not available to allow you to accomplish this, try volunteering for a while. Volunteer work is usually impressive on a resume. When necessary, comprise your heart's desire and work with different populations. It can be a good stepping-stone and may be more interesting than you anticipated. And remember, when you do get your first opportunity to work as a social work professional in the role of group leader of a support group or an educational group or possibly a therapy group, your *real* learning experience will have just begun.

9

MEDICAL SOCIAL WORK

∞CZ

Pamela Jenkins

Nature of the Work

Pediatric medical social work can be very challenging in some respects and very rewarding in others. We wear many hats. We are clinicians, mediators, advocates, educators, and case managers with a specialty in crisis intervention. As clinicians we do comprehensive assessments on all new patients. The assessment assists the social worker in identifying family strengths and challenges, their copings styles, social, financial, and psychological environment. It also identifies support systems, and if there aren't any, we assist the families in developing those supports.

Social workers assist families with adjustment to illness, the diagnosis and treatment, necessary interventions, and referrals. He or she should be able to assess child and family development. Social workers usually work with a treatment team that may consist of doctors, nurses, psychologists, and other supportive staff. The family and the team devise a care plan to be implemented for the patient as soon as possible. The social worker's role is to identify with the family any barriers that would inhibit the family from following through with necessary treatment. Unfortunately, many times the family may not disclose important necessary information timely, which places everyone in crisis intervention mode. This happens more often than not, especially with families that have limited financial support; the crisis mode becomes a way of life.

As a *mediator* the social worker assists the family and staff with an agreement about care by re-evaluating and revising the care plan throughout the patient's treatment.

Social workers act as *advocates* for families by recommending resources to provide ongoing support and assistance throughout the patient's treatment process, or for as long as necessary. We advocate for patient and family rights in the medical setting and in the community. We also try to ensure access to care is fair and equal and confidentiality is maintained. Social workers advocate and promote the needs of the socially, physically, and cognitively challenged. We try to ensure the needs of culturally diverse populations are met.

As *educators*, social workers often instruct the team how to effectively interact with the family. We educate patients and families informally and formally by teaching coping strategies and clarifying for them any information that may be confusing. The doctors will inform the patient and family of necessary tests and procedures. Although the physician may explain the procedure thoroughly, the clinical terms may be too difficult for many patients and family members to understand. The social worker or nurse is present to make sure the family understands what will happen. They also assist the family in making sure they ask the necessary questions before the tests happen. There are times when a patient or family member take on a more submissive role in the presence of physicians and are afraid to ask for clarification if they don't understand something. It is the social worker's role to intervene and assess the patient's level of understanding. It is also the responsibility of the social worker to educate colleagues about what's going on socially with the family, due to the impact barriers it can have on the proposed plan of care. Social workers also have the opportunity to educate other family members and friends, employers or colleagues, teachers or childcare workers, and the community at large.

The psychosocial implications of an illness can have a tremendous effect on the family, especially if the family has many other problems that need to be addressed. If the lifestyle of the family was chaotic before the diagnosis, many times it becomes worse after the diagnosis. Families function any way they know how in these situations. Many times they are not the way we might do things, but it is the only way they know how. So we as social workers have to start where the patient is, working with the strengths as a system and build on that. We should never be judgmental about families we work with because it affects the outcome, usually negatively. This is a very vulnerable time for patients and families when they are relying on the medical team to make things better. Trust becomes a tremendous factor for everyone involved.

Compliance can be a problem with many families if healthcare has never really been a priority for the family. Social workers can spend many hours trying to locate a patient just for routine and follow-up care.

Many social workers in a medical setting do individual, family or group therapy. This can include the patient, parents, family, co-workers of the diagnosed or classmates. The therapy is usually short-term or just a few sessions. If long-term therapy is needed it is usually referred to another mental health practitioner.

Social workers assess insurance and financial needs of the patient. If the patient has no insurance, referrals to financial counseling or the local Job and Family Services Department are completed to apply for Medicaid or appropriate insurance programs. Many families also need assistance in applying for social security benefits and Medicare. Social workers in hospitals don't take the applications, but we make referrals and assist families in completing the paperwork.

Discharge planning can be a major task for many social workers, especially those who work in adult care settings. This is truly case management service at its best. At times the social worker has a very limited time frame to arrange services before the patient is discharged. Those plans must be made and finalized upon discharge of the patient, especially if extensive home care is needed. Social workers are asked to complete many unexpected tasks with families because human behavior can be so unpredictable. In a medical setting you may find yourself doing impromptu marriage counseling, conflict resolution or setting up visitation for parents to see their child because they fight every time they're in the child's room together.

In the pediatric setting, school intervention services may be available for kids with a chronic illness. School Intervention is a service usually provided by a social worker in a medical setting, which focuses on assisting the ill child with getting intervention support services through the school if they have to miss classes on a regular basis because of illness. The social worker works with the child's teachers, school psychologist, counselor, and other appropriate staff to make sure the child doesn't fall behind because of missing so much school due to illness.

It is important for social workers to be informed about resource organizations in the community in addition to serving as a committee member with local agencies and volunteer organizations. Networking within these organizations allows the social worker to facilitate contacts and services, to expand services, and meet the wide variety of needs of patients and families.

If the social worker is working with a chronically ill patient, many times we have the opportunity to develop a relationship that is reliable and trusting. It is helpful to have this type of relationship in the event the patient must be transitioned from a long hospital stay to home care. Social workers must complete a full assessment regarding the patient and family support systems and the family pattern or style of living. The social worker would assist the family in identifying any barriers and helping to limit or eliminate any obstacles they might expect to happen.

In many hospitals or medical settings there are organizations that specifically provide services for patients with special needs. There may be special financial resources available, support groups or a special wish or dream come true organization that will grant a one-time wish. There may be special school services to assist the child in returning to school. In pediatric and adult settings there are programs for fun and socialization like special needs camp and exercise programs. There may be special activities such as parties, amusement parks, and sports outings.

Unfortunately, in the medical settings, many times with chronic and terminal illness eventually comes death. If the social worker and the rest of the team working with the family had a relationship, it will be difficult for everyone involved. As the social worker you console and comfort the family or refer for bereavement counseling while initially putting your own feelings aside, temporarily. You then console and comfort the team and make sure they have an outlet for their grief. Now it's time for you to grieve and the ideal situation is to grieve with your team. But what happens if you don't work with a team or it doesn't feel appropriate to grieve with your team? You as the social worker must have an outlet as well. You must be able to alleviate stress on a regular basis or it will lead to burnout. In most hospitals there are chaplains available around the clock. Also EAP services are always available.

Training and Degrees Required

My Bachelors and Master's degrees are in social work. I am licensed by the state of Ohio to practice social work only in this state. To obtain the licensure, the state administers an exam of 170 questions to determine the level of competency, only 150 of the 170 count. The others are practice questions. All questions have multiple-choice answers and there may be two or three right answers, but you must determine which is the best answer. The content areas consist of:

Direct Practice: Interventions with couples, groups, and families

Administration: Management

Human Development and Behavior: Theories, family functioning, and human development

Diversity: Culture, race, ethnicity, sexual orientation, age, and disability

Assessment, Diagnosis, and Treatment: Social history, identifying problems, assessments

Communication: The principles and techniques

Relationship Issues: The social and psychological factors

Professional Ethics: Values, ethics, confidentiality, and self-determination

Supervision, Evaluation, and Research: Collecting and analyzing data and utilizing research

Social work with other systems: Interdisciplinary planning and collaboration

Service delivery: Policy, procedures, and legislation. There is a fee to take the exam and you can take it as many times as you need to. If you don't pass the exam the first time you can take it again, but no more than three times in a year.

Personality Traits Deemed Important to Succeed

I believe the traits of personality one should have to become a skillful professional social worker are commitment to helping, self-respect, self-confidence and self-worth, patience, integrity, ability to get along well with others, empathic, hopeful, positive attitude, motivation, professionalism, ethical, good listener, observant, insightful, aware of one's own personal limitations, non-judgmental, compassionate, assertiveness, open-mindedness, and have an outlet for coping and relieving stress.

There are also professional characteristics and skills that will assist in the success of first class social work. Knowledge of resources and programs, social systems, how to access services, problem solving skills, competency, organizational skills, coping mechanisms, good communication skills, how to set goals and objectives, suggesting appropriate recommendations, assessment skills, interviewing skills, planning, evaluating outcomes, and follow-up. The professional social worker should understand boundaries and limitations, the hierarchy of needs for all humans, what concrete things that are needed to survive, which are food, clothing, and shelter. Be respectful of human diversity, the difference between cultural groups and individuals. There are also different lifestyles, choices, and chances; sometimes having access can make all the difference. I also believe in individualization. All persons should be treated based on their uniqueness.

Difficulties of the Work

There are many things that make this work difficult, whether you're working with an adult or child. I can remember conducting my very first interview as a professional social worker. I wanted to make sure I asked all the questions appropriately. I was on a home visit and my client was an elderly woman with cancer. She was a wealthy woman and not ashamed of anything anymore. I was young and eager to get this just right. When I arrived she was taking a bath, so her housekeeper let me in. She invited me into the bathroom to complete my first assessment visit. Needless to say the setting of the interview was not how I perceived it to be. It was distracting. It certainly caught me off guard. In time I learned to modify my assessment and interviewing skills according to the environment I'm in.

The goal of the first interview is always the same: you want to know why the patient is seeking your services. Let them tell you their story without you paraphrasing or interpreting for them. This needs to be their interpretation of the problem. Meanwhile you must continue to engage the patient, which can be very difficult. You also want to listen very closely and make sure the patient knows you're trying to understand.

In a pediatric setting some of the most difficult moments are determining whether a child has been physically abused, sexually abused, or severely neglected. Sometimes it's not always obvious by appearance. If the child is old enough you must interview the child about the incident or a history of incidents. We document when, where, how, by whom, and the relationship to the child. Medical neglect happens more often in pediatric settings than I care to mention. Unfortunately, if the parent leads a truly chaotic, disorganized life, that child and all the children become secondary to the chaos and disorganization. It's our job as social workers to assist the families with removing barriers within reason to allow them to be more compliant with medical appointments.

In the adult medical setting there may be patients in nursing homes, convalescent, and retirement homes who may experience emotional neglect. This may be due to no visitors, limited, no family still alive or sometimes family just getting so involved in their own lives they forget what it might be like to be in these settings and never receive a visit from someone who cares.

In medical social work deaths occur more frequently than any other type of social work. If you have problems coping with death and dying this is not the place. Social workers working in any setting must find a way to relieve the stress taken on in an average day. Although we are taught to leave it at the office, it doesn't always work. We are human and certainly have feelings. You will meet that one patient or family that touches you deeply. It will be difficult to detach once the relationship is over, but it must be done. If you find that attachment is happening too frequently, you are headed for burnout and you must remove yourself from the situation.

Another difficulty in social work is realizing you can't help everyone you come across. When I initially began working with families I wanted to help everyone I had contact with. It didn't matter the problem, surely there was a solution to it. What I found out is there is not always a solution to every problem. Some people are truly beyond that stage of another human being helping them. I then resort to prayer. I am a believer that God works miracles through people every day, but sometimes you must go directly to the source.

As a profession, social work is challenging, unpredictable at times, and never boring, but I find most people don't know what we do. Many people think we all work in child welfare. When I introduce myself for the first time to families, they may be defensive. So I must define my role as a medical social worker to the family and then bring those defenses down.

In a hospital setting the social worker rarely has a 9 to 5 day. Inevitably most emergencies seem to happen when you're packing up for the day to go home. There are many meetings to attend in this setting. You meet with staff, families, patients, and community organizations.

The case recording formats used in different medical settings are as follows. I am currently using the SOAP format.

SOAP

The **S = Subjective data** is about the problem as the patient views it. Is there a history with this problem and were there any prior attempts to solve the problem.

Then there is the **O = Objective data**, which includes the factual data along with staff observation of the situation. This would also include any testing results or even the patient's reaction to you.

The **A = Assessment** is next. This is your interpretation of the subjective and objective data shared with you. What are the risks involved? Assess the needs and the resources available to possibly help the problem situation. Also, what strengths does the patient have? What challenges might he or she incur as a result of diminished motivation?

Now the **P = Plan**. With the patient, define the interventions and treatment services needed and complete those referrals. Assist the patient in devising goals and objectives to carry out the plan. Then continue to follow-up with the patient. This may help him or her to stay motivated and follow through with the stated plan.

WORD Format

In some mental health settings the WORD format is used. This is used usually for follow-up meetings once the assessment has been completed and the plan mapped out.

W = Word, who, what, when, where, why, and **how? Who** is the patient and who saw the patient? **What** happened in the interview and who was involved? **Where** did the interview take place, in the medical setting or at the patient's home? **When** was the date and time of the interview? **Why** was there a purpose for the interview? **How** were interventions used to assist the patient?

O = Observations. Describe the patient in physical terms, emotional, psychological, and behavioral. If the patient has any control over the physical environment what is it like, then document it. The family interactions are also important and the patient's perception of the problem. There are topics of discussion initiated by the social worker, and the reaction of the family to those topics should be observed. Also get collaborative views from staff.

R = Reactions. What does the worker perceive to be the client's strengths and challenges? Document the progress of the treatment goals. What is the patient support system and family environment like? Are there barriers to reach goals? What are the ongoing problems and how can we revise the services to fit the needs? The social worker responds, completes referrals, and does follow-up with the patient.

D = Details of the next visit, meeting with the patient, is this a scheduled appointment, where and what time is the interview conducted. What would be the focus of the interview? Does the patient agree?

DAF or the Diagnostic Assessment Form

In other medical settings the DAF or the Diagnostic Assessment Form is used as the format of documentation. This form is utilized to assess the physical, mental, psychosocial, emotional, and cultural history of the patient. We document identifying information, describing the patient's gender, race or ethnic group, DOB, general physical appearance, occupation, and marital status. The next task is to identify the presenting problem and history of the problem. This describes the problem as the referral source and how the patient saw it. It describes the history of the problem, symptoms, and reason for seeking treatment at this time. We also ask about the length of time the problem has existed. We also want to know if the patient has had any previous success with interventions for the problem.

There is a mental status description given that includes appearance, behavior, stream or content of thought, the patient's affect, cognitive functions, and judgment.

The past psychiatric treatment history is important if there is one. In this instance we would want to know the age of onset, the duration and frequency of episodes, all hospitalizations and out patient treatment, the past responses to treatment, any medications prescribed, and how the medicines affected the patient.

Then there is the medical history. You must describe the medical hospitalizations and serious illnesses, any seizures, headaches or injuries. Are there any physical or developmental disabilities or special needs (i.e. interpreter)? We also need the name of the primary care physician. The current medication usage is important, as well as any allergies or sensitivities to drugs or dyes.

A cultural assessment is completed. This describes the patient's personal and family worldview, their healthcare belief system, and their religious and spiritual orientation. Who does the patient rely on for support in times of distress?

The patient's strengths, how have they coped in the past, and then assist with identifying natural supports to rely on. We also need to know weaknesses or limitations of the patient. What has been the biggest challenge for you to overcome?

The social worker then completes his or her assessment summary. This will include clinical impressions of the patient's current behavioral and emotional functioning. Also are there any indications that further testing is needed?

A diagnosis is given from the DSM-IV, which is the Diagnostic Criteria Manual. This manual identifies diagnostic codes and criteria, which describes mental health disorders, illnesses, and conditions. There is Axis I, which is the primary diagnosis. They are clinical disorders and other conditions that focus on clinical attention. The Axis II is personality disorders and mental retardation. Axis III refers to general medical conditions. Axis IV is the psychosocial and environmental problems. Axis V is the Global Assessment of Functioning, and whether the symptoms are mild, moderate, or severe.

Specific diagnostic criteria must be met for each Axis I through Axis V.

Rewards of the Work

There are significant rewards that come with helping people, which is what this profession is all about. Unfortunately, unpredictable human behavior can get in the way of the most perfect intervention and take you back to where the client wants.

In different medical settings the rewards can vary. As a medical social worker for children, I feel greatly satisfied when a child goes home in remission or cured of the illness. When I see a smile and a sigh of relief from the parent that a complicated procedure or test is over, and I'm there holding mom's hand as she holds her child's hand, I feel great when I'm working with a very chaotic person or family and we accomplish a goal we thought was extremely difficult to complete. Connecting with a patient or family you are working with sometimes can be challenging, but once that happens there is a bond that's difficult to break. As patients and family members come into the medical setting, it is a very vulnerable time for them. They are here because someone they care about is ill. They look for a lending ear or moral support from someone they can trust. Many times the social worker is the first person to make that connection. So your role becomes extremely important to staff and families because you may be the best source of interactive communication.

As a medical social worker working with adults I found the rewards to be quite different. Some of the adults thought of their illness as a "blessing" and not a curse. They started to appreciate life and family much more than they ever had before. Some mended severely decayed relationships they had with family members. Others discussed their appreciation for keeping things simple like enjoying the sunshine, gardening, and listening to birds chirping. Many just wanted to simply spend more time with family and had not thought of that as top priority before. This was truly a reward for me because it allowed me to receive the same rewards without having to experience personal illness.

I truly love social work because I believe it truly encompasses the holistic view of human behavior. We work with families to hopefully improve their social, emotional, psychological, environmental, cultural, and spiritual lives. I also believe without having a positive impact on all aspects makes the intervention more difficult, not impossible.

The field of social work is never boring and forever changing. There is always something fascinating about human behavior and you get to see a lot of it. Social workers are now also working in many different settings these days. We are in mental health, medical, child welfare, school systems, churches, private practice, psychiatry, community non-profit agencies, grief counselors, support group leaders, court systems, professors, research, and social policy, and the list goes on.

How to Get Started on This Career Track

I began my freshman year at an accredited institution in social work and majored in social service technology. I wasn't quite sure what I wanted to do, but I knew I wanted to help people live better lives. After two years I received an Associate degree and completed an internship. This gave me some real life experience helping me decide whether this was truly what I wanted to do. I then went on to receive my Bachelors and Master's degree in social work. If you're not sure whether this kind of work is for you, try volunteering in a non-profit community service agency. More often than not you will be working with people who are economically disadvantaged. You have to determine for yourself whether you can work with these populations being respectful and non-judgmental.

I do not regret in any way my choice to become a social worker, but I truly believe this work comes from the heart and if that continues to be the driving force, you will always be proud of your decision.

10

MINISTRY IN SOCIAL WORK

෨Ꮳ

Irvin Moore

Nature of the Work

Ministry is an area of social work practice that is seldom discussed. It includes social welfare agencies such as Salvation Army, Urban Ministry, Lutheran and/or Catholic Social Services, and other denominational social services. Some of these jobs are entry-level positions that require a Bachelor in Social Work (BSW). Social workers are afforded a wide variety of experiences in networking with other social welfare agencies, along with counseling individuals, families, and groups. These agencies require that a social worker have expertise in the field of interviewing and case management. Crisis counseling is also valued as an asset in many of these agencies.

We live in a pluralistic, multi-cultural, and multi-religious/spiritual society. In our social work programs, religion and spirituality are not subject areas found in the curriculum. There have been great debates about the separation of church and state throughout the centuries. Yet, the majority of Americans express some type of religious practice or belief. Religiosity is an organized institution where individuals gather to worship, pray, and find friendship; the institutions used for this purpose are called churches, synagogues, mosques or temples. Spirituality consists of beliefs, values or emotions in a higher deity, power or being. According to VandeCreek and Burton, "The word spirituality goes further and describes an awareness of relationships with all creation, an appreciation of presence and purpose that includes a sense of meaning."[1] The terms spirituality and religion are often used interchangeably, but they are not identical. R. P. McBrien points out that, "Spirituality is the way we orient ourselves toward the Divine. It is the way we make meaning out of our lives. It is the recognition of the presence of Spirit within us and a cultivation of a style of life consistent with that or presence. Spirituality provides a perspective to foster purpose, meaning, and direction to live. It may find expression through religion."[2]

An individual can be spiritual and not have an organized religion or faith group in which he or she belongs. A major question relates to how people of faith find employment in a non-secular social welfare agency? (The question that must be investigated is how do people of faith seek employment if they desire to work in a non-secular social welfare agency)? Chaplaincy is a type of ministry that helps to cultivate a person's spirituality and/or religiosity. It is hands-on experience in health care institutions, hospitals of all kinds (general, university, children's, psychiatric, military, and Veterans Administration), correctional institutions, geriatric centers, hospices, parishes, mental health facilities, industry, and a variety of other settings.

The professional chaplain recognizes the healing, sustaining, guiding, and reconciling power of an individual's religious faith or spirituality. Chaplains provide supportive spiritual care through empathic listening and demonstrating an understanding of a person in distress. Typical activities include:

- Grief and loss care;

- Risk screening—identifying individuals whose religious/spiritual facilitation of spiritual issues related to organ/tissue donation;

- Crisis intervention/Critical Incident Stress Debriefing;

- Spiritual assessment;

- Communication with caregivers;

---

[1] Larry VandeCreek and Laurel Burton, *Professional Chaplaincy: Its Role and Importance in Healthcare.* 2001, 3.

[2] R.P. McBrien, *Catholicism*, (Winston Press: Minneapolis), 1981, 4.

- Conflict resolution among staff members, patients, and family members;

- Referral and linkage to internal and external resources;

- Assistance with decision making and communication regarding decedent affairs;

- Staff support relative to personal crises or work stress.

- Institutional support during organizational change or crisis.[3]

The work of the chaplain may require interfacing with one or more of the above areas in his or her work setting. A chaplain's work can range from a generalist in a healthcare setting to a specialist in such areas as: Hematology/Oncology, Pediatrics, Psychiatry, Trauma, Transplantation, Decedent Care, and Intensive Care Units, to name a few.

Training and Degrees Required

In chaplaincy, a person should have an undergraduate degree (BSW). To enter chaplaincy an individual does not have to be "called" into the ministry (by call, the writer means to preach). However, it is important that the applicant maintain a level of spirituality or religiosity about himself or herself. Requirements for employment as a chaplain are a theology degree: Master of Divinity (M. Div.), Theology of Ministry (Th. M), and/or Master in Christian/Religious Education.

Unlike graduate schools of social work, all seminary students must start at the beginning level of their theological studies. It takes three years or 60 plus credit hours to complete a graduate degree in theology.

Many theological schools require one unit of Clinical Pastoral Education (CPE) as a part of a theological degree program. Clinical Pastoral Education is interfaith professional education for ministry. It brings theological students and ministers of all faiths (pastors, priests, rabbis, imams, and others) into supervised encounters with persons in crisis.[4]

---

[3] VandeCreek and Burton, 8.
[4] Taken from the ACPE brochure on Professional Education for Ministry—Clinical Pastoral Education. Decatur, GA, 1.

An individual is required to have completed a minimum of four (4) units of CPE. This requirement can be accomplished through a one-year residency in which an individual is enrolled in a CPE training program. There are over 350 accredited CPE training programs in the United States, consisting of hospitals, nursing homes, other medical facilities, military, correctional institutions, and industry. To enroll in a CPE training program the applicant must complete an application and submit an application fee. Interested persons can go online for an application at: www.acpe.edu. This is a helpful website for an individual to explore the various CPE training centers and locate possible residencies and employment opportunities and obtain other pertinent information about CPE.

Most CPE centers require completion of the first unit before applying for a one-year residency. Residency is a paid, full-time or part-time position with the average pay ranging from $22,000 to $27,000 depending on the center. The CPE process involves interacting with a peer group, didactics, supervision by a certified ACPE supervisor (faculty), and clinical assignments.

Personality Traits and Skills Deemed Important to Succeed

Clinical Pastoral Education affords the individual to do self-exploration of his or her own personality and family of origin dynamics. Utilizing a peer group experience, along with individual supervision, the individual is able to deal with the cultural developments that affect his or her pastoral formation. The heart of the CPE experience is his or her ministry with people and learning from that ministry through reflection, discussion, and evaluation.[5]

Using these same processes (seminars, peer group experiences, and self-exploration), the individual comes to terms with his or her personality as it relates to others. The CPE student/resident is enabled to evaluate his or her interpersonal, good communication, and intrapersonal skills as they relate to others. CPE is ministering and learning from several educational events. This experience ultimately affords the student the opportunity to evaluate chaplaincy as a possible career option.

In the workplace, an individual must be aware of his or her own religious and/or spirituality beliefs in that at times these beliefs may be challenged and/or called into question. A chaplain should not have his or her own "agenda" in doing chaplaincy. Most chaplains are considered as ecumenical

---

[5] Ibid, 3.

(non-denominational), as they will be required to minister to individuals from all religious and/or spirituality walks of life. Chaplains are discouraged from proselytizing and evangelizing. Further, a "messianic" mentality of trying to "save souls" is taboo in this work.

A chaplain must have a caring and genuine personality. These pastoral care providers enter this profession to serve others who are in crisis. Crisis counseling and crisis intervention are good assets in chaplaincy. Therefore, the way an individual responds or reacts to another person in crisis is very important. Chaplains should have an appreciation for the ministry and a desire to help others. A student/resident will discover that ministry is very broad and is not confined to the "four walls of worship." Openness to people from all walks of life is also an asset in this profession. Chaplains must be accepting of diversity (gender, racial, religious). Therefore, his or her approach should be non-judgmental. We all have biases and prejudices, but they must be put aside when called to minister to others.

Confidentiality is crucial in chaplaincy. A chaplain, in a very broad sense, can be viewed as a priest where the patient may confess his or her problems. As times have changed, ministers have relied on "clergy privilege" which has been tested in many courts. Once a degree of trust has been established, patients may disclose damaging information. Chaplains must also inform patients when safety concerns may require divulging such information (e.g. suicide, murder, etc.).

In line with confidentiality, the Health Insurance Portability and Accountability Act of 1996 (HIPPA) has brought about sweeping changes in American healthcare. There are strict penalties imposed on any healthcare provider, including chaplains, if an individual discloses patient information without authorization.

A good sense of humor is also recommended for this line of work. Since chaplains deal with life and death issues/cases, they must have an outlet for release of emotions. In pastoral care, that is called self-care. Self-care is the ability to find those resources that will provide sustenance and rejuvenation. Individuals are encouraged to seek some recreational or social outlets in this profession. It would be inappropriate for a chaplain to become obsessed in his or her work and therefore lose his or her level of judgment.

Perhaps the greatest personality trait for a chaplain is compassion. Joyce Rupp, noted author, discusses compassion. "Compassion has a price. It does not come without a cost, the least of which is the pain that pierces our own hearts as we accompany one who is suffering. When we speak out and take a stand against injustice, our compassion can cost us ridicule, rejection, loss of friends, and even the termination of our job. When we are willing to be present with one who is in great physical or emotional pain, our compassion can cost us our precious time and energy. Sometimes when we suffer with others, such as the homeless, the dying, those with AIDS, and the imprisoned, we can be confronted with our own fears, insecurities, powerlessness, arrogance, and prejudices.

Compassion urges us to move out of our comfort niches of security. Compassion stretches us and asks us to let go of apathy and indifference. Compassion refuses to accept excuses of busyness, ignorance, or helplessness. Compassion invites us to reach out to those who suffer, "to live," as Sharon Salzberg notes, 'with sympathy for all living beings without exception.'[6]

Difficulties of the Work

Ministering to people at their most vulnerable points in their personal or familial life cycle can be challenging. A chaplain enters into a person's pain and hurt. These are areas that the chaplain must remain attentive to and be present with the patient (customer). In chaplaincy, we identify this as having a "presence." Presence requires that the chaplain listen to what the person is saying and also (as something students in social work have been taught), to listen with the "third ear."

Chaplains enter the lives of patients and families at their most vulnerable points. In a crisis situation, a patient may react violently to some bad news and lash out at the chaplain. The job of a chaplain is to identify the patient's hurt and anguish in order to provide pastoral care. Many families are in shock from the sudden illness or death of a loved one. This may later take an emotional toll on the chaplain in dealing with continuous and/or subsequent crises.

Many think that the only job for a chaplain is to deal with death and dying. Death issues are just one of many types of pastoral care that a chaplain provides. The emotional heartbreak of a patient's death not only affects the grieving family, but it may also affect the chaplain. At times, a family may question the spiritual ramifications of removing someone from life support thinking that they are taking that person's life. The chaplain is present to help the family sort out their spiritual dilemmas in this area. Further, the chaplain may work with an organ procurement agency and the family concerning organ donations. The intensity of a death may stir up the chaplain's feelings regarding the death of his or her loved one.

---

[6] Joyce Rupp, *The Cup of Our Life: A Guide for Spiritual Growth* (Notre Dame: Ave Maria Press, 2002), 121.

To enter the pain and hurt of an individual is difficult. The chaplain may know how to get an individual "unstuck," but it is not his or her job. As pointed out earlier, the chaplain should not maintain any preconceived ideas about how this person is coping or not coping. Many view chaplains as "God's messengers" and believe the chaplains have an inside connection to help save their loved one. One of the shortcomings of this profession is for the chaplain to acknowledge his or her humanity.

Chaplains are encouraged to seek therapy. Therapy helps the individual stay in touch with his or her own feelings. The chaplain needs a professional to deal with unconscious and conscious experiences that may have occurred during the chaplain's childhood or other periods of his or her lifecycle development.

Rewards of the Work

When I was in seminary, one of my professors would overwhelm the class with an example that was very difficult and then say, "Anyone for law school?" A professional chaplain can question whether this is a profession that he is capable of doing. Chaplaincy is a very rewarding profession.

An individual may not always receive a "thank you" from a patient, family or staff member, but his or her work is appreciated. The majority of chaplain positions are in healthcare. The healthcare chaplain works with an interdisciplinary team consisting of: social workers, child life specialists, dietitians, primary care nurses, physicians, respiratory therapists, occupational/physical/recreational therapists, pharmacists, etc. As in social work, the interdisciplinary team provides a holistic approach to a patient's care and treatment. The chaplain is highly regarded among the interdisciplinary team because he or she can provide valuable insight into the spiritual and emotional health of the patient.

In 1998, the Joint Commission on the Accreditation of Healthcare Organizations (JACHO) made it clear that, "Patients have a fundamental right to considerate care that safeguards their personal dignity and respects their cultural, psychosocial, and spiritual values.[7]

VandeCreek and Burton cite numerous benefits for patients and families. They give five research area summaries that describe the benefits of attention to the spirituality of patients and family members. Due to the length of each study, the conclusions will only be summarized in this paper. (1) Religious

---

[7] VandeCreek and Burton, 3.

faith and practice impact emotional and physical well being. Professional chaplains play an integral role in supporting and strengthening these religious and spiritual resources. (2) Persons turn to spiritual resources during illness and other painful experiences, finding them helpful. Professional chaplains are trained to encourage helpful religious coping processes. (3) Professional healthcare chaplains play an especially important role identifying patients in spiritual distress and helping them resolve their religious or spiritual problems, thus improving their health and adjustment. (4) Families rely on religious and spiritual resources to cope with the high level of distress during a loved one's illness. A chaplain's care for family members has a positive impact. (5) Patients and family members are frequently aware of their spiritual needs during hospitalization, want professional spiritual attention to those needs, and respond positively when attention is given, indicating that it influences their recommendation of the hospital to others.[8]

How to Get Started on This Career Track

Just when you thought that once you received your Bachelor in Social Work (BSW), we're talking about adding on three more years of graduate education. A M. Div degree requires a minimum of 90 credit hours. As many are aware, the BSW is an entry-level job requirement. Where persons have this (BSW) as their immediate career goal, as previously pointed out, there are entry-level jobs if an individual has an interest in working in a non-secular agency.

For persons who wish to further their education, chaplaincy is a good opportunity. Again, however, it requires a Master in theological studies plus one year of CPE (residency). The challenge is one of dealing with paying off college loans versus adding more college loans to the mix. As in most graduate schools, seminaries offer scholarships, grants, and loans.

Theological school affords the individual the opportunity to gain a theological and a pastoral care theology. The majority of theological schools are denominational based. If an individual wishes to remain in his or her faith group, the starting point is to check with the local church for recommendations. Like most schools, campus tours can be arranged so the student can talk to faculty and staff.

While still in seminary, the student should take as many pastoral care courses as the school offers. In addition, a unit of CPE is recommended.

---

[8] Ibid, 11-15.

Some schools will give course credit when the unit is completed. Upon graduation, check the 350 accredited CPE centers and arrange for an interview if the student is interested in a residency.

If a person is interested in ministry, he or she should first talk with his or her clergy person. It is through this conversation that the prospective individual can determine if theological school is appropriate. If a person is interested, he or she should contact the Association of Theological Schools at www.ats.edu to get a list of seminaries.

Chaplaincy is a wonderful career. In actuality it is not a career, but a "calling" to do the work of ministering to those who are in distress, hurting or seeking answers to many of life's questions.

When I enrolled at Washington University (St. Louis, Missouri) in 1972, the graduate school of social work, along with other graduate schools, offered dual degrees. In the early years, an individual would take courses in two different schools to get a dual degree. Of note, the Southern Baptist Theological Seminary and the University of Louisville offered a dual (MSW and M. Div.) degree. However, these dual programs ended in 1995.

In 2002, the New Orleans Baptist Theological Seminary (NOBTS) received approval to offer an MSW. The seminary is pursuing the possibility of seeking accreditation from the Council on Social Work Education (CSWE) and appropriate funding. Presently, a student has the following options:

1. Enroll in the Master of Arts in Christian Education (MACE) program with a specialization in social work.

2. Enroll in the M. Div. program with a specialization in Christian Education and a concentration in social work.

3. Work on an MSW at the University of Southern Mississippi in Hattiesburg where an individual can take a few courses at NOBTS and get a degree in MACE and an MSW.

4. Enroll in a program related to social work (e.g. Marriage and Family Counseling) at NOBTS and get a Masters of Arts in Marriage and Family Counseling.

5. Enroll in an MSW program and, when the MSW program is approved at
    NOBTS, transfer to NOBTS.[9] Individuals can contact the seminary at 1-
    800-662-8701 or at www.nobts.edu.

Conclusion

Ministry and social work can be a rewarding and collaborative adventure.
Throughout the history of the social work profession, students have heard of
the separation of state and church. Yet, the church operated the early roots of
social services. President George W. Bush has promoted churches, synagogues, and mosques to deliver social services. More and more government
is trying to move away from doling out services to the poor and underserved.

Chaplaincy is an avenue in which an individual can incorporate social
work interviewing skills and techniques into pastoral care. Another resource-
ful attribute for chaplains is the networking that comes from being knowledgeable about social welfare and community resources to refer and/or consult with social workers on behalf of patients and families. Further, social
work and chaplaincy are concerned with empowering the individual. The
knowledge, value, and skills from both disciplines can only enhance the
competencies of a chaplain.

Bibliography

ACPE brochure on Professional Education for Ministry—Clinical Pastoral Education.
    Decatur, GA.
McBrien, R.P. *Catholicism*, Winston Press: Minneapolis, 1981.
Rupp, Joyce. The Cup of Our Life: A Guide for Spiritual Growth (Notre Dame: Ave
    Maria Press.) 2002.
Stewart, Liz. Office of Student Enlistment at New Orleans Baptist Theological Semi-
    nary. New Orleans, LA.
VandeCreek, Larry and Laurel Burton. *Professional Chaplaincy: Its Role and Impor-
    tance in Healthcare.* 2001.

---

[9] Information obtained from Liz Stewart, Office of Student Enlistment at
New Orleans Baptist Theological Seminary, New Orleans, LA.

11

ON BEING A PROFESSOR
OF HUMAN SERVICES

৪০০৪

Tuyen D. Nguyen

Nature of the Work

Professors of human services teach, research, supervise student research projects, present their research studies at conferences, publish their research articles in peer-reviewed journals, write books, and offer their expertise to their colleges/universities and occupational field through community services. Generally speaking, college professors do not have a typical 9 to 5 work schedule. For example, some professors like to have morning classes so they schedule all of their classes in the morning, which would then give them the rest of the day to engage in research, hold office hours, and so forth. Professors are employed at different types of colleges and universities. These types of colleges and universities determine the nature of the work that a professor is engaged in. There are the first-tier research universities where professors are primarily expected to be productive researchers, who publish on the average at least one research article in a prestigious journal per year. At these institutions professors are expected to teach two courses per semester and the emphasis is not so much on teaching as on research. Following first-tier research institutions are the second-tier research universities. At these institutions professors normally have a teaching load of three to four courses per semester. Research is still expected of professors who are employed by second-tier universities, but not as rigorous as first-tier research institutions. Within a five-year period, for example, professors at second-tier research institutions are expected to have published approximately 3-4 articles. At these universities emphases is on both teaching and research, with teaching taking a slight priority. Individuals who primarily like to teach and do very little research are usually employed by teaching colleges and universities, rather than by first-tier or second-tier research institutions. At these primary teaching institutions, students' learning is preeminent; therefore, having excellent student evaluations are crucial to professors in obtaining promotion and tenure at colleges and universities.

Before tenure is awarded to a professor, a faculty member holds the title of assistant professor of human services. The assistant professor is given six years to teach, research, and perform community service duties. After the six-year period ends, the assistant professor submits his or her portfolio in order to be considered for tenure and promotion. The portfolio normally contains published research papers, student evaluations, presentations, and community service accomplishments. The portfolio will be examined and approved by the department chair, the dean of the school, and the president of the university. If the assistant professor is granted tenure, he or she will be promoted to associate professor. At the associate professor level, the faculty member is then given another 5-6 years to work toward full professorship. However, some faculty members decide to stay at the associate professor level for the rest of their academic careers once they've got tenure.

In terms of teaching classes, some professors like to teach the same classes over and over again for years because they have developed an expertise in the area. As a result, their area(s) of expertise have become very focused over the years based on their experience teaching the courses and research done in the area. In a similar vein, some social science faculty members spend their whole academic careers researching the same topic(s) with some variations like with different ethnic populations in different environmental circumstances.

In short, the nature of the work for college professors of human services involves some basic elements including teaching, research, and community service for the university and the occupational field. The work schedule for college professors is mainly flexible, depending almost on when the faculty member wants to hold office hours, teach classes, do research, and so forth. However, untenured professors are given a fixed number of years to be productive in the areas of teaching, research and publications, and community service.

Training and Degrees Required

To be a college professor of human services, an earned doctorate (Ph.D. or Ed.D) in human services, counseling, psychology, or social work is required. Some institutions hire applicants with Master's degrees in a clinical field such as social work, and doctorates in fields such as gerontology, education or even law. Besides having a Ph.D., applicants for professorship positions in human services are also looked upon favorably if they also have post-master's professional paid practice experience in the field. A typical newly appointed human services assistant professor generally has at least 2-5 years of post-master's practice experience, either as a practitioner or administrator at some non-profit organization. In teaching human services courses, the emphasis is on integrating theory with practice, to make classes more interesting and applicable to students' real life practice situations. As a result, having field practice experience is the key to effective teaching in the field of human services.

Besides having field practice experience, newly hired assistant professors of human services also have to have "academic" experience such as teaching and researching in order for them to be marketable in the job market. Teaching experience can be accumulated during one's graduate studies, especially during the Ph.D. program. If one has taught a number of courses on a regular basis at the undergraduate and graduate levels, one's chances of getting hired as a tenure-track faculty increase tremendously. Last, but definitely not least, is the whole area of research experience and publications. On the average, newly hired assistant professors at research universities have ε᾿ ᾿erience in doing research either by himself or herself or with a professor 1 ntor while in graduate school. As a result of having research experience, ne   hires generally have one to two articles published or are in the process oι ʒing published by a peer-reviewed professional journal.

Personality Traits Deemed Important
to Succeed

Following are some of the personality traits that are deemed im   rtant to succeed as a college professor of human services. By all means the   ιre not exhaustive in any way. First, one of the personality traits deemed i ιortant to succeed as a college professor of human services, is the love of a uiring new knowledge (both theoretical and applied), about people and thei ςsues. This trait is crucial to the success of being a professor of human ser   ᾿es in the following way: effective professors are those who continually seek new knowledge, either through reading professional journals/books, attending conferences, or research; they easily capture students' interests in the class-room through sharing of their up-to-date knowledge. They are intellectually stimulated and passionate about the new things they are learning on a regular basis. Teaching is a way in which professors share their wealth of both accu-mulated and newly acquired knowledge with students. Dynamic and effective professors of human services are individuals with a thirst for knowledge about people, the struggles of being human, and interventions to alleviate human suffering.

Second, another equally important trait to be effective as a professor of human services, is the ability to disseminate knowledge that is understandable to others, both verbal and written. Learning new things is excellent; however, an effective professor must be able to communicate what he or she knows in a clear and precise manner in order to pass on the knowledge to others. Being able to break down complex principles and techniques into simple terms that others could understand is a trait of an effective communicator.

Last, successful and content human services professors who have been in the field for 20-30 years possess a trait of collegiality. These professors know how to create positive relationships with their colleagues; departmental duties and power are normally shared among human services untenured and tenured faculty members. These individuals know the importance of having good relationships with their colleagues within the department for the purposes of support, working on same projects, and sitting on the same committees. Some of these individuals have to work side by side with one another in the same department for 20 to 30 years. Therefore, the ability to build positive collegial relationships with colleagues within the same department is a personality trait deemed important for those inspiring to be professors of human services.

Difficulties of the Work

One of the difficulties in becoming a college professor of human services is obtaining the required degrees and credentials. An individual first spends four years to earn a Bachelor's degree (e.g. human services, psychology, sociology, social work). After earning the Bachelor's, an individual then goes to graduate school for a Master's degree (e.g. MA in human services, psy-chology, MSW in social work). After earning a Master's degree, an individual may opt to collect supervised practice hours (usually takes 2-3 years) for licensure as a licensed therapist, social worker, or counselor. A lot of individuals take a break from school at this point and immerse themselves in their careers for a while. Some work in the field for 20 years while others take 5 years before returning to school for their doctorates. The doctorate usually takes four years to complete (15 additional courses beyond the Master's degree and a dissertation). All graduates of accredited Ph.D. programs have to complete a dissertation, a large research study conducted by each graduate under the supervision of a tenured professor.

Once a person is appointed a professor he or she has to continually keep updating his or her knowledge of the field through reading and attending conferences. A difficulty in achieving this task may lie in the fact that the professor has to juggle with a wide range of activities: teaching classes, supervising student projects, conducting his or her own research, writing articles, granting writing, presenting and attending conferences, and serving on committees. A person has to learn how to manage time and switch gears as needed, for example, from writing an article for two hours then to teaching a class of 25 students on a topic totally different from what one has been thinking about for the past two hours. Furthermore, one has to switch from an introverted activity such as writing an article to being an extrovert in a matter of minutes in order to teach and interact with students well in a classroom. In short, being flexible to play different roles and able to manage one's time well is the key to overcoming the difficulty of juggling with various tasks and updating one's knowledge of the discipline.

One of the difficulties of having a career as a professor in a research institution is publication. Professors at these institutions are expected to publish in prestigious well-established journals. And getting your articles published in these well-known journals is extremely difficult. For example, some journals will accept only 3 percent of the total number of manuscripts submitted on a yearly basis. Less prestigious journals will accept up to 15-30 percent of the submitted manuscripts. If one's article has been accepted, usually it is required that an author makes revisions suggested by reviewers before the article is to go to press. Getting good publications is a difficulty that almost all professors at research institutions face. For those untenured professors at first and second-tier research institutions, a minimum number of publications have to be met within a 5-6 year period in order for tenure and promotion to be awarded.

Rewards of the Work

There are a variety of rewards in being a college professor of human services. The following are some of the major rewards:

- Once an assistant professor receives tenure and promotion to associate professor, he or she will have job security for life. The university guarantees the tenured professor that under ordinary circumstances (no major budgetary problems or criminal acts on the part of the professor) he or she will not be laid off or fired. Tenure protects college professors so that they can have the freedom to write and publish on any topic areas they wish for the sake of knowledge building. It is rewarding for a professor to know that once tenured he or she no longer has to be concerned about job security. The job basically is theirs for life!

- Professors have ample opportunities to study, build or extend knowledge and disseminate it through publications; this can be an extraordinary reward. Further, professors not only disseminate their research studies through publications, but they also present them at national and international conferences. They get to travel to places and the university usually pays for their travel expenses.

- Professors feel rewarded when they teach students, especially on topic materials that are their expertise areas. What is more rewarding for professors are when they witness students having an "a-ha experience" in understanding and connecting materials lectured in class. In short, one of the rewards, which professors enjoy in their profession is teaching and passing on knowledge to others in the classroom.

How to Get Started on This Career Track

If one is an undergraduate in college, he or she can choose a social science field as a major to build the foundation and have the prerequisites needed for graduate studies later on. Make sure one has taken courses such as introductory psychology and sociology, research methods, statistics, abnormal psychology, and human development before one finishes an undergraduate degree. Strive to maintain a strong Grade Point Average (3.0 + GPA), as an undergraduate because one's overall GPA will play a huge role in determining one's chances of being accepted to graduate school. As an undergraduate, try to get connected with a professor whose research areas one is interested in and see if there are opportunities where one can work with him or her as a research assistant. These opportunities in working with a professor on research projects expose one to conducting research and getting published. Some professors would list their undergraduate research assistants as second authors on their journal articles. In a similar vein, for every writing and research assignment in one's classes, always regard it as a potential publishable journal article. Seek the advice of the professor teaching the course of the possibility of publishing one's completed assigned project.

In the first semester of one's senior year, deciding on which graduate school to apply for a master's program is critical. Factors to take into consideration for this task include the prestige of the school, finances, location, requirement of admission test, and the curriculum involved. Prestigious schools will have higher demands and expectations on incoming graduate students, and it can be extremely expensive to attend these institutions. One can have a lot of debt upon graduation if one decides to attend an institution with high prestige. On a more positive note, if one earns a doctorate from a university of high prestige, one's chances of getting hired by a prestigious institution as a professor increase dramatically. This is a personal decision that an individual has to decide for him or herself.

Once in a master's program, an individual can decide which human service specialty one wishes to pursue, from mental health track to human service administration, depending on the type of graduate program. Further, while in the master's program, an individual will have opportunities to engage in internships that require a total of 400 to 600 clock hours. After earning a master's program one can then work toward licensure hours to become a state licensed social worker, mental health counselor, or marriage and family therapist, depending on one's Master's degree.

The last educational endeavor which one has to partake to be a college professor is earning a doctorate. The majority of the accredited doctoral institutions require the Graduate Record Examination (GRE) to be taken by doctoral applicants and the scores have to be five years old or less. A doctoral curriculum normally requires 15 graduate courses beyond the master's level and a dissertation. There are departmental comprehensive examinations, verbal and/or written, over both core and specialty courses which one has to pass in order to proceed in the program. After one passes all the qualifying examinations, the next phase of the doctoral curriculum is the dissertation. First, a dissertation committee has to be formed by the doctoral student. This is simply done by the student asking one tenured professor to be the chair of the committee, and four to five other professors to be members. Usually these professors' research areas are closely related to your dissertation topic. The topic of the dissertation first needs to be proposed and approved by the committee before one can start working on it, like collecting data. The doctoral student and the chair of the dissertation committee work closely with one another over an extended period of time. The dissertation usually takes one to two years to complete, depending on the topic and committee involved. Once the dissertation is complete and with the approval of the chair and committee members, the student proposes a date to defend his or her dissertation. At the dissertation defense, the whole committee listens to a doctoral student explain his or her dissertation, step-by-step, of what was done and the conclusions drawn from the research. The committee will then have opportunities to probe and ask the student questions regarding different issues of the dissertation, from methodology to the results of the study. The last part of the dissertation defense is the committee's recommendation to either unconditionally pass the student's dissertation, pass with revisions, or fail. If the student successfully defends his or her dissertation, committee members will congratulate him or her with the title of "Doctor" and regard the new Ph.D./Ed.D. as a potential colleague.

12

PROBATION OFFICER AS A CAREER CHOICE FOR SOCIAL WORKERS

ഓരൂ

Samuel S. Faulkner

Introduction

This chapter will provide an overview of both probation officers (sometimes referred to as Community Supervision Officers) and parole officers. It will review the differences and similarities in the two positions, discuss the nature of the work, some of the difficulties and rewards of the work, and provide information on how to be hired as a probation or parole officer. The author also provides some insights as to the various settings where probation and parole officers are found (both traditional and non-traditional settings). In addition, this chapter will discuss the differences between working for the state and federal governments.

Nature of the Work

A probation officer and a parole officer are two different entities. Each performs a separate set of duties, though there are some common tasks in their jobs. Probation officers supervise individuals who have been sentenced to probation. Probation is usually given as a sentence in lieu of jail time. A person sentenced to probation serves a predetermined sentence, usually with conditions set by the court, and when their time on probation is over, nothing further is required. People who are on parole are those who have served a jail sentence and been released from prison before their sentence is finished. A parolee reports to a parole officer on a prearranged basis. The parole officer tracks their compliance with pre-set conditions like obtaining employment, submitting to regular drug testing or attending drug treatment counseling.

There are two types of probation officers—those who work with juveniles and those who work with adults. Rarely, in small, rural jurisdictions, a probation officer may work with both adults and juveniles. However, this would be considered the exception rather than the rule. Both have common goals—to protect the public, assisting offenders in obtaining gainful employment and living useful lives, and helping those convicted of crimes become productive citizens and refrain from committing more crimes. Probation officers supervise those on their caseloads through personal contact with the individual and their family members. Many probation officers will schedule appointments with people on their caseload to meet at the probationer's homes or place of employment. Regular, unscheduled visits to a person on probation in their home or on their job is not uncommon. Probation Officers routinely seek information from other individuals to collaborate information about how the probationer is doing. Church groups, the probationer's therapist, other counselors, employers, family members, and friends may all be potential sources of information for the probation officer. Probation officers may arrange for ancillary services such as drug rehabilitation, counseling, vocational training, or anger management classes for those on their caseload.

Probation officers spend a considerable amount of their time working for the courts. They are responsible for investigating the convicted individual and preparing a report for the judge. This report is known as a Pre-Sentence Investigation. It guides the judge in sentencing by providing information about the person's job history and employment skills, family history, level of criminal involvement, and drug use history. Before submitting the report the Pre-Sentence Investigation (PSI) is usually reviewed with the offender and their family. Officers may be asked to give recommendations to the judge as to sentencing for the offender. Later, the probation officer would be required to appear before the judge to testify as to the offender's compliance with the conditions of probation and attempts at rehabilitation.

Parole officers perform essentially the same functions as the probation officer. However, the parole officer is hired by the state, whereas the county hires probation officers. The parole officers are responsible for providing supervision to those on parole, monitoring their compliance with conditions for their release (obtaining employment, remaining free from the use of all drugs, attending counseling sessions, etc.), and making reports to the court and prison system regarding the parolee's progress.

The counties of each state, on the other hand, employ probation officers. Most counties have separate departments for adult and juvenile probationers. Correctional Treatment Specialists (sometimes referred to as Case Managers) work in prisons and jails. They serve much the same function as probation officers providing supervision to inmates. The main function of the Correctional Treatment Specialist, however, is to help the inmate plan for their release. Correctional Treatment Specialists may also be found in parole or probation agencies. They provide reports to parole boards when an inmate is being considered for release. Other duties include working with inmates to help them obtain counseling (such as anger management treatment, drug rehabilitation, counseling for sexual perpetrators) or linking the inmate with vocational counselors or other rehabilitation specialists to prepare them for release.

The size of the caseload that a probation officer carries depends on several factors. These include: the level of supervision of the offender, the risk the person poses to the community, and the amount of ancillary services needed by the individual. Caseloads, then, can vary from as low as twenty, to as high as 2,000 individuals. New and emerging technologies such as a fax machine, electronic monitoring, computers, and drug testing allow the probation officer to carry ever-increasing caseloads. Part of the probation officer's duties includes determining the level of supervision an offender requires. Criminals are assigned a level of supervision that is based on a formula. The supervision formula includes the level of violence involved in the crime, number of prior crimes, the crime itself, the overall social history of the individual, and other factors. Training in assessing level of supervision is provided after a probation officer is hired. Probation officers, once hired, receive between 40 and 80 hours of specialized training that leads to state certification as a probation officer.

Parole officers, as a general rule, have smaller caseloads. Caseloads range, on average, from about 80–150 active cases. The smaller caseloads are the result of the more intense supervision required by each person on parole as opposed to those on probation.

Training and Degrees Required

A minimum of a Bachelor's degree is required to obtain a job as a probation officer or Correctional Treatment Specialist. A degree in Social Work, Criminology or Sociology is required. However, a degree in Social Work makes the potential probation officer highly marketable because of the undergraduate training in case management, group facilitation skills, basic counseling, and documentation. Advanced graduate work and a Master's degree in social work are always desirable qualifications. Some states require a Master's degree or experience or some combination of both. A Master's degree is also often a prerequisite for being considered for advancement or supervisory positions. Many officers are hired on a probationary status and can work for up to twelve months before completing probation and being hired in a permanent position. As stated earlier, after being hired, each state provides its own training for its probation and parole officers. Yearly, ongoing training is also a routine part of the job.

Juvenile probation officers are found only at the state level. The federal government has no juvenile parole officers, only federal probation-parole officers. Positions as federal parole officers are considered to be highly desirable jobs. The caseloads are much smaller than those of the state probation officer and the pay is considerably higher. However, to be hired as a federal parole officer a person must first work as a state probation officer. There is no set amount of time, but federal parole officers all have experience as probation officers before being hired by the federal government.

Personality Traits and Skills Needed
to Succeed

This occupation is not for everyone. It requires a certain degree of physical stamina, and because the nature of the work is in close proximity to criminals and dangerous neighborhoods, the probation officer needs to have the ability to make decisions, think critically, and act decisively. Anyone with a felony conviction would not be eligible for this job. Probation officers, parole officers, and Correctional Treatment Specialists need to have excellent writing skills, be knowledgeable about computers, and have a fundamental understanding of laws and regulations surrounding corrections. Many states ask potential employees to complete a written, oral or psychological exam. Drug testing is also a routine part of the hiring process.

Other desirable traits include being in good physical condition and possessing a degree of maturity. The ability to endure insults, angry outbursts, and emotional displays are all part of dealing with individuals who have been convicted of crimes—many of those individuals have little or no social skills. Probation officers often have to ignore individual's behavior and not lose their temper while simultaneously setting limits and being firm with an offender. It is not uncommon for someone on probation or parole to feel discriminated against, anxious, nervous or depressed. A probation or parole officer needs good listening and counseling skills as well as knowledge about community resources.

Difficulties of the Work

Probation officers and parole officers are officers of the court. It is their duty to enforce court orders. This means that at times the officer must make arrests, perform searches, seize evidence, and arrange for drug testing. In addition, the probation or parole officer must follow-up with those on their caseload. This involves home visits (often in dangerous neighborhoods). Due to the dangerous element that is regularly encountered by the probation and parole officers in some counties, probation and parole officers are required to carry a firearm.

Probation officers are regularly required to attend court hearings and proceedings. They are asked to make recommendations about probation violations and sentencing for offenders. Parole officers routinely attend parole hearings and make recommendations about their clients.

It should be noted that both probation and parole officers work with all age groups regardless of the population they are assigned to supervise. Juvenile probation officers meet with parents, school officials, and other service providers on a routine basis. Adult probation officers have regular contact with spouses, children, and other family members in the course of their day.

Rewards of the Work

As with other human service professional jobs, probation officers and parole officers have intrinsic rewards that are not always tangible. The reward of helping an individual return to society and obtain gainful employment is hard to measure.

Case Example: Tony was a 37-year-old African-American male when he was released from prison for armed robbery. Tony had few job skills, was functionally illiterate, and his prospects were dim. However, his parole officer saw something else in Tony—a natural ability to relate to people. Tony was encouraged to attend adult basic literacy classes and learn to read. With the encouragement and a gentle shove from his parole officer, Tony interviewed for a position as a paraprofessional counselor working with skid row alcoholics and drug addicts. Tony's credentials as an ex-con and natural ability to listen to people made him an excellent counselor. Within two years of Tony's release from prison, he had obtained his high school equivalency degree and enrolled in the local community college. Tony continued to work as a counselor and attend classes at night. He eventually completed an Associate's degree in Substance Abuse Counseling and went on to obtain a Bachelor's degree in Social Work. Tony died at the age of 48 from complications due to diabetes. However, he accomplished something in his life and more importantly, he made a difference in the lives of those he worked with—all because someone believed in him.

Probation and parole work is difficult. The high recidivism rate for those returning to jail can be disheartening. However, there are rewards in the job. Tony is an example of someone getting out of jail and turning his life around. For Tony, the system worked. A probation officer or a parole officer can make a difference.

How to Get Started on This Career Track

The best way to be hired in the field is to begin early. If you are a student, now is the time to start making contacts. As you complete your undergraduate degree in social work, begin to take some classes in Criminology. Arrange to complete a practicum placement at a probation office. One of the most effective ways to help get your name and face known to a potential employer is to complete what Richard Bolles calls an "Informational Interview." You make an appointment with a probation or parole officer and interview them. Prepare questions ahead of time and ask such things as:

- What do you like best about your job?
- What do you like least about your job?
- What are the working conditions like?
- What can I do to prepare for a career in this field?

The informational interview serves several purposes: it gives you information about the potential position, it will help you to decide if this is a career you are interested in, and it helps to establish job contacts for later on. When you do interview for a position as a Community Supervision Officer, you can talk knowledgeably about the position and the strengths you would bring to the job.

Summary

Being a probation officer or parole officer can be an exciting, demanding, career. It offers the opportunity to make a difference in an individual's life. It, too, can be demanding and challenging. Probation officers are found in all fifty states and the Department of Labor predicts this will be a field that will continue to grow and have a positive job outlook for the foreseeable future. Probation officers report that despite high caseloads they like their jobs. If you are an individual who enjoys a relatively fast-paced job with the opportunity to work with a variety of different people, then this may be a career that would appeal to you.

13

SCHOOL SOCIAL WORK

℘℘

Seth Knobel

Your experience as an intern will be different than
your experience when you get hired, which will be
different than your experience in any other school.

— Paraphrased from Karen Rolf,
school social work professor extra-
ordinaire

Individual therapy, group therapy, crisis intervention, member of pupil
personnel teams, social developmental studies, social histories, *crisis
intervention,* Individualized Educational Plans (IEP), Manifestation Developmental Plans, in-service trainings, workshops, parent meetings, re-entry meetings, *crisis intervention,* meetings with parents, deans, administration, teachers, community leaders, community agencies, outside therapist, psychologists,
and psychiatrists, did I mention *crisis intervention?*

School social work is a unique profession, which encompasses many
different aspects of social work: community, agency, administrative, and
policy. The experience of being a school social worker will be different depending on which of the three levels of academia one works: elementary,

middle or high school. Those experiences will also be different in rural versus urban communities, as well as state-to-state.

In general, an elementary school social worker will likely be the only social worker at that school. This position may be part-time or may be split amongst several schools. Due to limited resources, facilitating supportive group therapy will make up a large part of the job. Groups could include, friends groups, children of divorce, low self-esteem, loss of a parent, etc. Seeing students individually for therapy will be rare. Individual sessions of one to three sessions at most will be mostly assessment based and "checking-in" with students to gauge how they are doing. Being an elementary school social worker will also require working directly with teachers to determine classroom accommodations for students that are having trouble. A significant responsibility in an elementary school setting will require the completion of social developmental studies. Social developmental studies are a process that determines whether a student is eligible for special education. Most students with a learning disability will be found during their elementary or middle school experiences. It is unlikely that students develop or are discovered as having a learning disability at the high school level.

Middle school social work experiences will be similar to elementary. Developmentally, students are changing at a more rapid pace. Issues that students encounter are different than in elementary schools. Doing mixed gender groups may be appropriate for some students in primary grades. During pre-adolescence conducting male or female specific groups will prove to be more productive. Some areas of concern today in middle schools are anger and increased usage of drugs. Teaching anger management skills and conducting "explore your usage" groups are implemented at the middle school level. Students begin to date in middle school; therefore, groups on healthy relationships or peer pressure are important. With more issues facing students, a middle school social worker is required to conduct more groups, yet seeing students individually will also be required. Adopting a brief treatment model with limited and solution focused sessions will allow a school social worker to see more students throughout the year. Conducting social developmental studies are still a large part of the job, as well are disability plans. Meetings with teachers and parents to implement classroom accommodations will increase. Due to a larger number of students to service making referrals to outside agencies will be necessary. Also at this level, as at the elementary level, there may be no other school social workers in the school or even in the district.

In high schools, social work involves all of the above to the nth degree, but this is a time developmentally when students are dealing with more emotional issues. Identifying learning disabilities and eligibility for special education will still be an issue, but emotional and behavioral disturbances will be seen more. Issues of ADD and self-esteem often become more apparent than in younger children. Spending time in parent meetings, sometimes just to explain the nature of normal adolescence will be beneficial. It is also at this stage of academia when responsibilities are split between special and general education. At the high school level there is often more than one social worker, both in the district and even in that school. In these cases, many different models of school social work may be implemented. A school social worker may be solely responsible for special or general education students, and some may have responsibilities in both.

Nature of the Work

As school social workers, we have a mantra, a philosophy, a mission statement that represents the actual nature of the work that we do. At all of the three levels of schooling the mantra is the same:

> *As a school social worker your main responsibility is to pro-vide support for students who are having **difficulty in school** due to attendance, economics, health, emotional, and/or family problems.*

A school social worker supports students with issues, which prevent them from being successful within the school environment. It is commonplace to work with students who have behavioral problems, family issues, academic failures, underachievers, substance abuse problems or issues of pregnancy. During a 30-year plus school social work career, there will be few issues that will not be addressed at some point.

Within a school environment, the school social worker becomes the liaison between the school, home, and community and provides services that link them together. In 1992, the board of directors of the National Association of Social Work adopted 33 standards for school social work. Among these standards are a code of ethics, seeking outside supervision, and continuing education through workshops or advanced degrees. A complete list of the standards can be found at http://www.socialworkers.org/sections/credentials/school_social.asp.

What We Do For Teachers

For teachers, we provide consultation and assist in creating accommodations and strategies for classroom management. Many teachers have limited knowledge of specific disabilities and even less information on how to accommodate these students. School social workers help teachers by educating them about disabilities and brainstorming with them on how to implement accommodations in their classroom.

A common problem, which all teachers encounter, is a student who is being disruptive in class. A school social worker would observe the class to evaluate how the student's environment might be altered to help the student. Sometimes the solution is as simple as rearranging the student-seating chart. A student who is distracted by their location in the classroom may be able to concentrate more easily in a new seat. For example, a student with ADD sitting next to a window will find it difficult to concentrate on the lessons at hand when there are more stimulating things going on outside of the window.

What We Do For Students

There are the three rules of working with students: *Support, Support, Support.* School social workers help support students, whether working with a student individually, conducting a group, creating classroom accommodations or helping change discipline policy. Each of these strategies is designed with the idea of how it is going to support students.

Crisis intervention is a significant aspect of a school social worker's job. No matter how organized, how prepared for the day one is, there is always a crisis. A crisis can be a torturous break-up between the two most popular students in school. In either middle or high school this can not only involve providing services to the couple whose relationship broke up, but may involve other students who become so distraught over the break-up that they cannot compose themselves in class.

Another all too frequent crisis is a student who threatens to commit suicide. When working with students at all levels, you must assess whether the student is in danger of hurting themselves or others. Making referrals for an outside psychiatric evaluation or bringing a student to the hospital is another aspect of the job. At times, you may have a student who has stopped taking their anti-psychotic medication and once again hears voices telling her to kill all those people who are wearing red. Getting this student immediate help from outside sources will allow you to get the services needed to help that student and their family.

Other crises may come from the community, a deadly house fire, murder of a student's parent, a car accident, or the death of a teacher. In these cases, often the school social worker will work with social workers and counselors from the community to provide services.

The most important thing to remember about a crisis, is that one, it is unplanned. Therefore, putting off a report until the next day, thinking there will be plenty of time, may prove to be wrong.

Conducting groups is another aspect of the work, which allows a school social worker to provide services to more of the school population. There are far too many students who need services and even though all of them might benefit from individual work, there is hardly enough time and/or resources to accommodate all of them. Learning to prioritize and determine which students require individual sessions and which can be managed by group sessions is an essential skill that needs to be learned. When social workers examine their student caseloads, they may discover that five students are confronting the same issue like interpersonal skills. Combining those students into one group will free other time slots, as well as provide ample opportunity to help those students practice their interpersonal skills.

Working with students individually at some schools is seen as an impossibility, while at others it is the foundation of social work. With an increase of mental health issues among students, social workers are expected to provide mental health services. Having good clinical skills is necessary to provide much needed help to students. In many schools, the social workers' schedules and responsibilities only allow them to work with students during an assessment period. Other schools pride themselves on the "Cadillac" service of providing private practice work within a school environment. Depending on one's interests and skills, one should seek out a school that fits them.

What We Do For Parents

Parents are sometimes confronted with a school system that is quite overwhelming. Providing them with a road map of the system is extremely useful. This is especially true in the area of special education. Spending time with parents, explaining the process, and its benefits will often improve their ability to help their child.

Many parents find themselves unprepared for raising children. Assisting parents with parenting skills is another aspect of school social work. Through

both one-on-one contact and in small group formats describing normal adolescence to parents and sometimes teachers are important. For example, a
parent concerned that their son is a heroin addict because he came home with
blue hair is not an unusual phone call for a school social worker. By helping
parents understand these issues both the parent and child are helped.

Making referrals for families to outside agencies and therapists is a major
component of school social work. Some students will need individual work
that can best be provided by a community agency or private practitioner. A
family may need resources to assist them in acquiring basic services (e.g.
food, clothing, health insurance, social security, housing, financial assistance,
or employment). Usually communal agencies are the most appropriate places
to provide these services.

An Example of Working with a Student

In my present job in a high school, I worked with a student, Krissy (not
her real name) who has many emotional problems. After an extensive outside
consultation with a psychologist, it was determined that she was suffering
from Dysthymia with schizoaffective tendencies. This student's level of anger
was so great that just walking into the class produced her saying "Get out of
my bleeping way." Even if we were successful in helping her get to class,
remaining in the class was another problem. To help this student, I explored
three possible avenues of help, the student herself, her parents, and her teachers.

I began seeing this student on a weekly basis, providing supportive counseling work. After three weeks, I had contacted the parents and sent out
teacher comment sheets. After meeting with the student's parents, I learned
that many of these same behaviors had been seen at home. It had only been
recent that these behaviors were being seen at school. When I recommended
outside therapy to the student, I was not surprised when I was met with a
resounding "No bleeping way." I believe the echo from that student's statement still rings faintly in the halls of the school. As a result, one of my first
goals when working with this student was to create a therapeutic alliance that
she trusted and so that together we could explore the possibility of outside
therapy. After two months of weekly sessions, she agreed to attend outside
therapy.

Providing this student support in school became a major challenge not
only for me, but also for her teachers, dean, and academic counselor, not to
mention the student herself. Working as a team, we met weekly to discuss this

student, as well as others. We came up with a plan based on all of our past experiences and created new accommodations that we thought would help this student be successful. First, we agreed to continue with individual work. Even though she was going to see an outside therapist, we agreed that she continued to need additional support within the building. Second, we also provided her with a timeout pass. This pass allowed her to leave any class or school function, at any time, to get a drink of water, take a five-minute break, go for a hallway walk or seek out a member of the team; social worker, academic counselor or dean. Then, after a discussion with the student and her parents, we decided that we needed to meet with her teachers.

When meeting with the teachers we decided an early morning meeting with coffee and bagels would be best. Number one rule when working with teachers is to always feed teachers at early morning meetings. We started the meeting by asking them what types of behaviors they were seeing with Krissy. Then we spoke with them about Dysthemia, schizoaffective tendencies, and bi-polar (at this point, this was a possible diagnosis). We explained the nature of these disorders, how they might manifest themselves in her behavior, and then discussed ways to address them. Through our discussion, we realized that she gets extremely overwhelmed in large groups. The science teacher suggested, with the help and permission of his department head, that Krissy work on her own within the classroom. As long as she was producing the same amount of work as other students, he had no problem when the assignments would be turned in. This proved to be very successful. Krissy, being as intelligent as she was when motivated produced several days of work in a single class period. This allowed her to choose one day a week off, permitting her to have an additional weekly period to "decompose (her word)." We also provided ongoing support to the teachers helping them realize that her comments were not intentional statements of disobedience or a personal attack on them. This enabled them to stay connected and empathic to Krissy, aiding them to build trusting relationships with her.

Through our work with the student individually and our consultation with the outside therapist, we discovered how much the parental behavior contributed to her level of frustration and how it triggered negative behavior. After several parent and pseudo-family therapy sessions (as school social workers we do not do family therapy), we recommended that they seek out outside family therapy. They agreed, and with a list of potential places, they followed through on family therapy and things improved. The parents understood how they contributed to their child's behavior and Krissy learned to identify triggers that set her off.

After working with this student for a year, providing individual work both inside and outside of school, family consultation, family therapy, weekly team meetings, quarterly teacher meetings, classroom accommodations, and a cooling off pass, she improved but still required more emotional support than the general education program could provide. The team, which included the student, parent, academic counselor, and dean discussed and agreed that a Social Developmental Study was needed to determine whether she was eligible for special education services, thus providing even more support for her. After the process, it was determined that she was eligible for special education. She is now receiving a special education resource class that is helping provide daily academic support. She also has a few accommodations to help her with work completion. For example, she can take all tests and quizzes by herself, she can work independently in class, she can choose if she wants to do group projects, and she can interview teachers before selecting her schedule. With these accommodations and continuing with the others, we hope, we can help her be successful.

Training, Degree(s), License Required

Each state is different, so it is best to contact the Department of Regulations in your state. Most states will require some sort of certificate or license. At a minimum a Master's degree in social work is usually preferred. In the State of Illinois, both a Master's degree in social work and a Type 73 certificate are required. This certificate qualifies a school social worker to work with special education students. There are two specialized classes required for this certificate. One is a class on gifted students, which will give a thorough background on children with disabilities. The other class is advanced school social work, which prepares students to write Individualized Educational Plans, Disability Plans, and gives a background on school systems. The other requirement is a yearlong internship within a school. This internship is usually three days a week. If one is placed in an elementary school, it is a good idea to visit and possibly spend a week or two in the other two levels of academia. If available, one should experience how to do a social history of an elementary and a middle school student.

A school social worker will be doing different things at different degrees depending on their school. Having different experiences will help when interviewing for jobs and deciding where one's interests and skills lie. If there is any interest in working in a school during your career, it will be easier to fill the above requirements when working toward a Master's degree, rather than after graduation and already working in the field.

Other licenses that may be required are the LSW, Licensed Social Worker, and the LCSW, Licensed Clinical Social Worker. The LSW can be taken as soon as a BSW has been earned and may be required in various fields of social work. The LSW has a licensing exam issued by the Association of Social Work Boards. The LCSW can only be acquired with a Master's degree in social work and 2000 post-clinically supervised hours, as well as passing a licensing exam. Many schools do not require an LCSW when starting, but may want their social workers to work toward it.

Personality Traits and Skills Deemed Important to Succeed

When working in any system, one needs to learn to be flexible, organized, and patient. When moving up the developmental ladder of trials and turbulent times, different skills may need to be applied. For example, in a high school environment crisis intervention and mediation skills can be extremely helpful, if not a necessary component of the job. Learning how to work with parents is also an essential skill. You can always help someone want to change, you can even help someone to change, but it is difficult to maintain that level of change if their environment doesn't change with them. This means working with the parents. Many schools do not do family therapy, but having a few sessions with a family may prove to be extremely important. If they need more than just two sessions, then a referral to an outside agency may be your next step.

Knowing your community resources is extremely important. What agencies are out there? What are they doing? Which person is in charge of what programs, services, funds, etc.? What are the needs of the community? Doing a need assessment will prove invaluable when identifying where you plan to put your energies. It would be a waste of time and resources if there were an agency in the community that does great work with drugs and alcohol, than for a school social worker to be creating a program from scratch, especially if they are willing to bring their services into your school.

Writing is another skill that is important to have. With the agency that comes into the school, they may want to collaborate on a grant to continue or expand their services in your school. Grant writing skills then become very helpful. Other areas of writing that are necessary are process notes, social histories, and communicating with teachers and staff. Writing presentations for explaining disabilities or getting teachers on board through a workshop on reduced homework assignments for students with short-term memory loss disabilities is also useful.

Being creative will go a long way within a school system. From juggling an impossible schedule, to creating a new group, being creative will keep things fresh and ever changing. When working with transfer students in a high school, we offered many services. Unfortunately, many of our transfer students didn't take advantage of these services. We found, though, that many of our transfer students were at school usually 30 to 45 minutes before school began. After speaking to a few of the students, we learned that they were not interested in services being offered during the school day because it interfered with their academics, as well as their socialization time. And after school many of them had to leave school immediately to take care of younger siblings or had to get to work. But the majority of them were there earlier because many of their parents started working early and they were being dropped off at that time. But many were here early to have a government-subsidized breakfast. So what did we do? We provided services weekly in the morning starting at 6:45 A.M. with a 7:30 A.M. school start. And by the way, we also offered them breakfast.

Program creation is another great skill to have as a school social worker. Learning how to do a need assessment, create a program, and then implement it will help you be successful at any level.

Knock Knock. Who's there? Boo. Boo who? Don't cry it's only a job. Okay, granted, bad joke, and horribly altered to bring up my next two points. A sense of humor is critical. Being a school social worker is a difficult and an emotionally draining experience. Whether telling a family about their child's disability, trying to alter a student's behavior or telling a parent that we have to hospitalize their child for suicidal ideation, is all difficult. There are three lessons that are important to learn when working as a school social worker. One, have a sense of humor. Having a sense of humor will help break up all the emotional baggage the students bring to sessions. Two, learn *not* to take the job home. Allowing time to rejuvenate is important. Do an impromptu research project. Next time when visiting a school around the holiday break or two weeks before summer vacation, find out how many staff are out sick. Sometimes it is not just the flu that's making people feel bad. The third lesson is to take care of you. If you don't have outside interests beyond school social work, *you will burn out.*

Difficulties of the Work

The hardest part of the job is the bureaucracy. When working in a large system there are many people with really good intentions. Sometimes those good intentions clash with others' good intentions. When working with a student with oppositional defiant disorder who told a teacher to "Bleep off," a disciplinarian, assistant principal or dean, would say, "Suspend the student." A social worker may see this as an opportunity to help the student realize what had happened, what went wrong, what was their part in the situation, what they did could affect others, and hopefully work with them to discuss other alternatives of what they could have done. It is difficult to do this with a student who is now out, what the student would call a ten-day vacation. There should be consequences for this student's action, but maybe those deterrents could be done within school, so that the student, who probably isn't doing well academically, can still be in school being supported academically and emotionally.

Another frustrating aspect of school social work is the limitations of the work that can be done. As stated earlier, many schools don't have a family therapy component. This can be a critical foundation needed to help a student.

It is difficult to fully process certain issues with a student long-term when working with a student whose parents are divorcing or someone who has discovered that they were molested as a child. It may be inappropriate to send that student to English class after 40 minutes of processing this in a session. Making some accommodations to the work is extremely important.

Depending on the school and its resources, there may only be one school social worker. This can at times make for a very lonely job. If you are able to be creative and solicit and train teachers to co-lead groups, one may be in a position to create an entire department of paraprofessionals.

Another difficulty is the never-ending feeling that there isn't enough time. A school social worker spends a lot of time putting out fires and creating interventions. Inevitably, things get put aside. Sometimes that means not taking a lunch, coming in early or staying late, and sometimes taking work home. Understanding one's limits will come in handy. Learning when to say, "Not Tonight," and starting fresh the next day, helps everyone.

Rewards of the Work

Being a student today is difficult. And being a parent trying to raise that student is sometimes even more difficult. As a school social worker you are in a position to help support those efforts. Schools are a central component to our communities. It is the only institution that will affect every person in that community. Therefore, schools are being asked more and more to provide services that have not typically been seen as a school's responsibility. Many schools today have begun running food pantries, organizing clothing or winter jacket drives, or started a clothing closet. Many schools hold community health fairs and organize employment expos. To be a part of these efforts helps make real change in the community.

The other obvious benefit is working with students. Schools are made up of unique, diverse, and special people. They have hopes, dreams, and passions. They are depressed, confused, and unmotivated. They are excited, driven, and self-confident. As a school social worker, being able to guide and foster all of these efforts, at all different levels of academia, is rewarding. Remember, it is a school social worker's job to help students deal with those issues that get in the way of them being academically successful. And because of this, the job is critical to any school.

Working in a school environment allows a school social worker to support and advocate for students. Students struggle daily with issues that affect them academically as well as personally. To be in a position to help students through difficult times has great rewards. I have seen firsthand how a life can be changed or in some cases saved. Working with a student who is suicidal, or one who has an addiction to drugs, or a pregnant teenager are just a few of the experiences that a school social worker may face. These are critical moments in a student's life and they will need someone with the knowledge, skill, and desire to help them.

How to Get Started on This Career Track

In any profession it is important to know your limitation. Do you like working with young kids, teenagers, urban versus rural kids? Do you want to work with gang-infested communities, low economic issues, or culturally diverse communities? The list goes on and on. Taking time now to decide which population you work best with is a good start. Many people start in community social work before they enter into schools. They learn needs assessments, build case management skills, learn program creation, and work with families. These are all skills that can help in schools. The best advice is to take advantage of your youth and volunteer everywhere. Get to know different organizations, populations, and the programs that help. The best volunteer experience is to become a tutor. As a tutor, learn how others learn.

This can be extremely helpful when trying to come up with accommodations in the classroom.

Conclusion

Being a school social worker is a wonderfully rich experience. It is a profession that includes aspects from various fields. To be successful one must use skills from agency, community, private practice, and administrative social work. The job is difficult, but truly rewarding. It is a great place to spend a 30-year career.

14

SOCIAL WORK CAREER PATH
AS A PROGRAM EVALUATOR

℘℃℞

Cynthia A. Faulkner

Introduction

One of the emerging career opportunities for the social work professional is that of Program Evaluator. Two separate and distinct phenomena have emerged to create this necessity for professionals who are trained evaluators. The first is the need for the profession of social work, as a whole, to be more accountable. Starting in the late 1960s and continuing through today, there has been an increased emphasis on being able to demonstrate results through rigorous, scientific methods. Changes in the profession led to a philosophy that social work needed to be able to prove its effectiveness. It has become increasingly important for the professional to be able to demonstrate results using both qualitative and quantitative methods. As stated above, the evaluation of practice has become one of the most important aspects of the social work profession. Both undergraduate and graduate programs are teaching students the basic principles of evaluating practice. Tools such as the Single Subject Design and Program Evaluation are regularly taught in classrooms today.

The second issue is the decline of funding sources. As funding streams have dried-up, the social worker and agencies alike have been pressed to demonstrate fiscal responsibility for grant monies. Today, all federal grants, and many state grants require an independent evaluator to be designated at the time the grant is written. Agencies like United Way and many private foundations are mandating some type of evaluation to be included in the grant process. The Program Evaluator acts as an auditor to determine if goals and objectives are met.

This chapter will examine the role of the Program Evaluator as a possible career path for social workers. It will explore the nature of the work, training and degrees required, and the positive and negative aspects of the job. In short, it will help you to gain some insight into this particular aspect of social work and decide if this sounds interesting to you.

Nature of the Work

Program Evaluation is a broad category that may seek to answer a variety of questions:

- Is this program helping clients?
- How many people are we serving?
- Are we meeting our objectives?
- Is there a better/more effective way of providing these services?
- How can this program be improved?

The Program Evaluator is in the unique position of helping social work professionals to examine their programs. It seeks to take an honest, evaluative look at the services being provided. Program Evaluators work with administrators, Executive Directors, direct service staff, and administrative staff in the course of their duties. Evaluators often interview other, ancillary people who are important to the program's existence. These may include: consumers, staff of other agencies, and other professionals in the community.

In short, Program Evaluation involves working both independently and with groups of people. Because the evaluator often is hired as an independent consultant, the individual who chooses Program Evaluation as a career needs to be self-motivated and able to work independently. And, because the nature of the work means giving feedback to the agency, it is necessary to develop skills of tact, diplomacy, and to be able to communicate well.

When working as an outside evaluator for an agency who has received federal grant monies, it is important to realize that many times, grant agencies impose short timelines for reports. For example, it is not unusual for a federal grant to require a quarterly report to be due fifteen days after the end of a quarter. If a quarterly funding cycle ends on March 31, it would not be unusual for the granting agency to require a quarterly report due in their office by April 15. This means an extremely short time to enter and compile data for the report. Evaluators, then, are often called upon to meet strict deadlines with little room for flexibility.

Training and Degrees Required

Program Evaluation, by nature, requires an individual to possess good "people skills." An individual who works as a Program Evaluator will encounter many different types of people (often in the course of the same day) and it is imperative that the evaluator be able to listen, give feedback, ask pertinent questions, and seek out information in a tactful manner. Skills inherent in the counseling process are also called into play in the evaluation.

In addition to the ability to communicate effectively, Program Evaluators need to have an understanding of research methods, including both qualitative and quantitative procedures. Evaluators also need a solid grasp of statistics and statistical procedures.

Because Program Evaluators are often independent consultants hired by the agency to conduct the evaluation, a certain degree of education and credentials are essential. For this reason it is recommended, but not always required, that a Program Evaluator hold a Master's in Social Work (MSW). The MSW training also provides a thorough understanding of statistical procedures, Single Subject Design, and a basic grounding in research methods. For the individual wishing to pursue consulting work as a Program Evaluator, it is suggested that whenever possible, working with experienced evaluators is an excellent way to train for the job.

Other training that would be helpful would be to take classes in basic marketing and business management. Working as a Program Evaluator means essentially functioning as an independent businessperson. Knowing how to market yourself, advertise your business, and how to keep records are always useful skills. It is also important to investigate the laws in your particular state regarding social workers and private practice.

Personality Traits and Skills Deemed
Important to Succeed

Most individuals who have advanced to the level of professional social worker (either through the process of completing a Bachelor's in Social Work degree, or by obtaining a Master's in Social Work degree) will possess the necessary skills and personality needed to be a Program Evaluator. However, this is not to say that just because someone possesses the ability and temperament to be an evaluator that it will appeal to him or her. This job is for the individual who prefers a challenge, is well organized, and likes to work independently. It requires a personality type of someone who is self-motivated, disciplined, and able to make decisions. As an independent consultant it is important to know basic marketing techniques and how to advertise.

In addition, the person who would be successful as a Program Evaluator needs to be able to think critically (be able to possess good judgment), have excellent analytical skills (the ability to separate into component parts or elements), and think logically (the ability to reason). These skills also need to be coupled with excellent people skills: the ability to listen, to communicate effectively, and to be assertive when necessary. Some may believe that these traits are mutually exclusive, but in reality they are not. They are simply the skills of a well-trained social worker.

Difficulties of the Work

Program Evaluation is no different than any other job. There are aspects of the job that are enjoyable and some that are pure drudgery. However, most people who make their living as Program Evaluators (or who supplement their income with part-time consulting work) report that the work is both challenging and rewarding. The process of assisting an agency in clarifying goals and objectives, and developing clear methods for meeting them is inherently rewarding. It is always pleasurable when working with an agency and you can report that consumers are satisfied with the services and they feel the organization is doing a good job.

Conversely, it is never pleasant to have to report negative results to an agency. Some Program Evaluators have been pressured to slant or even change results to be more favorable to the agency. This is where the skills of tact, diplomacy, and assertiveness are most useful in order to remain ethical in reporting findings.

Program Evaluators, who work as independent consultants, report both positive and negative aspects to their jobs. It is nice to be able to set your own schedule, work when and if you want, and take time off without having to worry about punching a time clock. However, the downside is that money can be sporadic. It takes discipline to manage money when there is not a guaranteed income at regular intervals. Another downside to being a consultant is that instead of one boss you have multiple bosses—all clients become your bosses, and all can make specific deadlines and demands on your time.

How to Get Started on This Career Track

Getting started in the field of Program Evaluation is often the most difficult part of the whole process. One of the best ways to begin is to work with an established professional evaluator. This may entail working as a data entry clerk or other associated tasks, but it is an excellent way to learn the ropes.

Another way to break into the field is to work within an agency and serve as part of an evaluation team. Taking classes in Program Evaluation, while completing a degree program, is another excellent way to begin gaining experience. Volunteering to work as part of an evaluation team or working with professors as a research assistant are other ways to break into the field. Once you have proven your energy, ability, and willingness to work hard, professionals will be willing to recommend you to agencies they work with.

Once you have gained some initial experience, word-of-mouth and self-promotion are the best ways to get your name known. Let your clients know that you are seeking other customers. Offer to provide initial evaluation services at reduced rates, in return for a good reference or recommendation. These are all marketing techniques that help new businesses to get established.

Marketing, however, is a key to the establishment of any new business. It is imperative to find out who the consumers are in your area. Ask friends and colleagues to recommend you to their agencies. Find out who is writing grants and ask if they need an evaluator. Talk with your local United Way Office and begin to develop a relationship with their staff. Place a small ad in newspapers, company newsletters, and church bulletins. Be creative, but remember personal contacts and self-promotion are often the best forms of advertising.

How Lucrative is Program Evaluation

The author does not want to portray Program Evaluation as the golden goose of social work. On the other hand, it can be a profitable enterprise as a contractor. Federal grants awarded to an agency in a large metropolitan city can be rather large: $500,000 per year with the Program Evaluator receiving 10 percent or $50,000 per year. To be fair, not all federal grants are this big, nor do they include that much for evaluation. But it is not out of the question for an evaluator to charge a sum per hour that might equal a private practice session. In addition, many evaluators hire less-skilled assistants to do data entry. This can generate hourly income more than triple the hourly wage and is a way to begin to learn the process.

This is not to say that you will always be paid such a princely sum for your work. Much depends on the size of the grant, how well known you are as an evaluator, and your reputation for competent and honest work. Additionally, if you are working within an agency conducting program evaluation, your salary is your payment and the experience you gain is a valuable asset for independent and/or part-time work.

Summary

Program Evaluators are a new and emerging sub-category of social workers. Program Evaluators work as independent consultants or within the agency for which they are employed to help agencies determine their overall effectiveness. They work with agency staff, board members, clients, and others in the community to determine whether the program is meeting its goals and objectives.

It is not mandatory, but highly recommended, that an individual who wants to pursue a career as a consultant should hold an MSW degree. In addition, it is highly useful to have completed classes and training in both program evaluation and statistics.

Those who wish to be successful, as Program Evaluators, need to have excellent interpersonal communication skills, as well as the ability to think critically, and problem solve.

Working as an independent consultant—whether as a Program Evaluator or in private practice, is both frustrating and rewarding. The independent businessperson has the freedom to set their own schedule, work when and if they want, and take time off as desired. The downside is that money is often sporadic. In addition, marketing a business and self-promotion are not one-time events, but on-going enterprises that must be constantly engaged in to ensure a steady supply of new customers—especially for the first few years until a business becomes well known and a solid reputation is established.

Program Evaluation is an emerging field of social work. It promises to have expanding possibilities for the enterprising professional who is self-motivated and energetic. While not for everyone, this career choice is an excellent opportunity for the individual who enjoys a challenge and works well with him or herself.

15

THE SOCIAL WORKER AS POLICY ANALYST

∞ဢ

Patricia Newlin

For professionals wishing to expand their experiences in the private sector to have a greater impact on policy making, a somewhat unique position is the social worker as a policy analyst within an array of public agencies. Likewise, there are opportunities for professionals with public sector experiences to broaden their impact on policy making as a federal policy analyst. This chapter will address the role of the social worker in federal agencies with a focus on the social worker as a policy analyst in child welfare.

Definition of Policy Analysis

Dunn (1981) defined policy analysis as "an applied social science discipline, which uses multiple methods of inquiry and argument to produce and transform policy-relevant information that may be utilized in political settings to resolve policy problems" (p. 35). Majchrzak (1984) defined policy analysis as "research done by political scientists interested in the process by which policies are adopted and the effects of the policies once adopted" (p. 104). Bovbjerg (1985) made the connection of the concept to the public in his definition: "Policy analysis is systematic thinking about public issues or decisions leading to practical responses that can be broadly communicated" (p. 154).

Definition of Policy Analyst

In his study about policy analysts in bureaucracies, Meltsner (1976) described the function and role of the policy analyst as follows: "The policy analyst is an advisor, and policy analysis is advice" (p. 50). Some examples of the policy analyst work according to Meltsner (1976) include "short-term...responses to unanticipated inquiries" (p. 54), "contract coordinator" (p. 57), "writer" (p. 63), "studies: on top and in teams" (p. 65), and "evaluator" (p. 69). How the advice of the policy analyst is used can be described as "decisional and supportive" (Meltsner, 1976, p. 73). For example, a policy analyst could develop alternatives and recommendations to address an issue or problem relating to an existing policy or proposed policy in the former or provide rationale for a specific policy decision in the latter.

The Social Worker as Policy Analyst in the Federal Government

Policy analyst functions in the federal government can be found in an array of civilian and military agencies and levels with varied titles, e.g. management and program analyst, social science analyst, budget analyst, operations research analyst, policy analyst, program analyst, lead program analyst, and program specialist. They include such functions as policy/program reviews; evaluation; conducting studies; analyzing policies; developing policies or revising; state plan developers and evaluators; advice to legislators, states, universities, local communities, agency managers, other agencies, policy teams, contractors, or managing grants. Policy in the federal government can relate to statutes, proposed legislation, Executive Orders, regulations, and an array of formal standardized policy instructions and interpretations within individual agencies.

Although many of the functions and job titles that describe the policy analyst do not require social work degrees, several of these functions are consistent with descriptions of social workers roles related to policy. Haynes and Michelson (1997) described the social workers' role influencing policy related to "documentation" ("gaps, barriers, social problems, unmet needs"), "testimony", "expert witness", and "written communication" (pp. 75-78). In

2001, Ginsberg identified a difference between counselors and social workers are that the latter also may be "working with (and as) policy makers" (p. 9).

Ginsberg's description of social workers in the macro arena as follows complements functions of the federal policy analyst: "As part of their professional responsibilities, social workers develop programs that assist people to prevent or solve problems, develop and promote legislation, and otherwise deal with larger systemic concerns" (Ginsberg, 2001, p. 9).

Policy Analysts in Federal Child Welfare

Policy analysts in federal child welfare are located in the Department of Health and Human Services which is one of those agencies employing social workers Ginsberg (2001) referred to as "administrative agencies...that administer the government social welfare and social services programs" (p. 111). Other such administrative agencies that might attract social workers include The Department of Labor, The Department of Housing and Urban Development, The Department of Justice, The Department of Agriculture, The Peace Corps, The Executive Office of the President, and the Department of the Defense (Ginsberg, p. 111).

In practice in the field of federal child welfare, an analyst or program specialist will consult with many of these federal administrative agencies, as well as states, communities, tribes, universities, voluntary agencies, and other stakeholders to coordinate national policy, initiatives or goals, or to address issues.

Nature of the Work

Social workers as policy analysts at central offices in Washington, D.C. or surrounding areas can have more targeted, specialized jobs than their counterparts in federal regional offices currently located in ten offices, e.g. Boston, New York City, Philadelphia, Atlanta, Chicago, Dallas, Kansas City, Denver, San Francisco, and Seattle. For example, policy analysts in the central office could design evaluation components and evaluate specific national data sets, e.g. adoption, child abuse and neglect, adoption or foster care. Other policy analysts could interpret legislative intent and analyze and develop regulations and policy or perform budget analysis and forecasting for legislation or regulations. Some policy analysts could be researching the impact of crack cocaine on caseloads compared to the impact of newly developing methamphetamine and other critical issues impacting the child welfare population. Policy analysts participate in an array of program reviews of adoption, foster care, and in-home programs with their federal regional partners and other stakeholders.

Regional policy analysts may be identified as program specialists with an array of policy analyzing functions including the following: activities related to expert advisor regarding policy including federal statutes, regulations; joint planning in state plan development, including training plans; monitoring; program/policy reviewing, evaluation, and program improvement; grants development, approval, evaluation and management; policy review, development and implementation; review and comment regarding General Accounting Office studies, Health and Human Services Audits, Office of Inspector General Audits or Program Assessments; and special projects or initiatives. The program specialist as a policy analyst may perform all of these functions related to a specific assigned state and perform some specific functions as a regional expert. Some policy analysts in regions may have fiscal analysis functions to ensure statutes, regulations, or other policies are properly managed as part of their program specialist jobs or as a separate function.

As a regional program specialist performing policy analyst functions develops expertise or brings prior experience or training to the position, the specialist may be requested to add duties as an expert in policy work groups, special initiatives, lead for joint planning, other policy development, e.g. adoption, waivers, public hearings, legislative committees, national initiatives, program reviews, state plans, working with National Resource Centers, state or regional work groups, planning conferences, working with management consultants and universities, in an array of child welfare related issues.

An example of a regional policy analyst (as a program specialist) interpreting and developing national policy is the response to a public inquiry about an undisclosed retroactive latent disability of an adopted child. The parents had adopted what they thought was a "normal, healthy infant" and therefore did not require a federal adoption subsidy. If the disability had been known prior to the adoption, the child would have been considered a "special needs child" and would have been eligible to receive a federal subsidy. The regional specialist social worker not only worked with necessary federal and state agencies to ensure this child qualified for a federal adoption subsidy, but also hundreds of other children through helping the central office policy writer develop the national policy.

In another example of a regional social worker policy analyst (as a program specialist) developing national policy, a regional policy analyst was temporarily assigned to the National Policy Work Group on Family Preservation and Support in Washington, D.C. to develop policy and a regulatory base to implement the Family Preservation and Family Support Services legislation (title IV-B, Subpart 2) which was part of the Omnibus Budget Reconciliation Act of 1993 (PL 103-66). Policy analysts participated in an array of focus groups of child welfare experts, e.g. child welfare directors, judges, providers of family support services, and advocacy groups to gather and analyze information for use in developing policy guidance for implementation of the statute. Work group members individually conducted research through interviews, review of legislative history and committee reports and drafted brief issue papers defining the specific programmatic, fiscal, planning, legal and administrative issues; background; alternatives and recommendations. The team periodically met with highest-level federal officials to discuss their individual analyses and overarching guidance, e.g. guiding principles, vision, collaboration, systems change, collaboration, new partnerships, and exemplary programs in developing the new policy guidance.

Social workers as policy analysts in regional offices may participate in other National Work Groups through conference calls, electronic discussions, research and suggested revisions of policy guidance or regulations related to child welfare training, title IV-E Foster Care and Adoption State Plan or the comprehensive community, state, federal partnership known as "joint planning" of each state's comprehensive Child and Family Services Plan (CFSP). Likewise, policy analysts provide expert advice about child welfare policies (e.g. major legislation) through public hearings, legislative and community meetings, developing conferences, and leadership roles in promoting national initiatives, e.g. Youth 2000 Initiative, White House Initiative on Employer-Sponsored Child Care, National Hispanic Services Delivery Assessment Initiative, Healthy Marriage Initiative, Rural Initiative, Faith-Based and Community Initiative, National Foster and Adoption Family Recruitment Campaign, and the National Foster Care Review Initiative.

Training and Degrees Required

In the section regarding personality traits and skills, pursuing the Master of Social Work (MSW) degree, especially macro specialty and experiences in field placement, was suggested as excellent training for a federal policy analyst. Agency support of graduate and postgraduate education varies by agency and location.

Although the MSW degree is not required for a policy analyst, an MSW and state agency experience have been preferred during various organizational and political environments for program/policy analysts in the federal child welfare arena. In the past, substitution of the Master of Social Work or Doctor of Philosophy degree for experience has varied by job and location. For social workers with an MSW who are seeking a license or advanced license (or certification depending on state), the challenge may be to find a supervisor with both an MSW and appropriate social work license.

Personality Traits and Skills Deemed Important to Succeed

Ginsberg (2001) summarized "key attributes" for social workers working in federal agencies classified as "administrative agencies" as follows: An interest in and talent for social work administration and macro or larger system practice..."(p 112). Policy analysts specific skills include advocacy, analytical, evaluative, advisement, negotiation, organizational, administrative, policy analysis, writing, oral, team building (leadership) and membership, creativity, sense of timing, planning, and research skills.

Social workers as policy analysts are able to build on their Master of Social Work (MSW) degree especially in research, statistics, community practice, planning, administration, and policy. Many universities have infused child welfare content across the social work curriculum especially children and families areas of concentration and/or those with title IV-E training contracts with state agencies. Policy analysis in the foundation policy courses and the advanced policy courses, e.g. child welfare policy, provide a strong background for using models for analysis including defining problems or issues, history, alternatives, and recommendations. Policy classes in an MSW program strengthen the policy analysts' ability to review and analyze regulations, policies, legislative histories, committee reports, and federal/state statutes necessary for developing position papers or issue papers used for recommending policy changes whether they are statutory, regulatory, or other policy/program changes.

Research and analysis of federal major legislation such as the Adoption Assistance and Child Welfare Act of 1980 (PL 96-272); Omnibus Budget Reconciliation Act of 1993, Title IV-B, Subpart 2, Family Preservation and Support Services (PL 103-66); Adoption and Safe Families Act of 1997 (PL 105-89) provide content and analytical skills for becoming a policy analyst.

Other child welfare legislation such as the Child Abuse Prevention and Treatment Act, Chafee Independent Living Act, Multiethnic Placement Act, the Indian Child Welfare Act, and other parts of the Social Security Act that address child welfare training and research and demonstration are useful content areas.

Practice experience or field placement in state child welfare agencies or non-profit agencies providing services to families and children in the child welfare arena are good sources of experience for becoming a policy analyst in federal child welfare. Knowledge of resources and research available from National Resource Centers related to foster care and permanency planning, special needs adoption, youth, organizational improvement, child maltreatment, and others is useful for a policy analyst. Likewise, knowledge of research available from the federal child welfare agency, General Accounting Office (GAO), Office of Inspector General (OIG), and private key national, non-profit organizations such as Child Welfare League of America (CWLA), American Humane Association (AHA), and American Public Human Services Association (APHSA) related to development, evaluation, and implementation of programs; policy; staffing (recruitment, retention, training) standards; information systems/data, and training.

Difficulties of the Work

Policy analysts need to be cognizant of the variances of the political, social, and economic environment of policy making. The Adoption Assistance and Child Welfare Act of 1980 (PL 96-272) was a major child welfare reform bill enacted with bipartisan support and issuance of timely proposed potentially meaningful implementing regulations. Early in the rule making process, the political climate changed to an anti-regulatory environment resulting in significantly delayed final regulations that were of limited use to key state policy makers. During the decade of implementation of this child welfare reform, numerous policy guidance and interpretations were necessary. Even the monitoring/review processes during this period lacked regulatory authority.

With the passage of the Omnibus Budget Reconciliation Act of 1993 (PL 103-66), policy analysts, with extensive internal and external stakeholder input, developed and issued timely policy guidance allowing preliminary implementation within approximately six months of enactment. This legislation created the new "capped entitlement for family preservation and support services and earmarked amounts for evaluation, research, training, and technical assistance; state court assessments and Indian tribes" (Newlin, 1997).

During the last twenty years, there has been diminishing resources for programs at the regional office level. This limits operational travel and attendance at professional conferences. Special initiatives change in scope and may reprioritize limited resources.

Rewards of the Work

The social worker as policy analyst, positively affecting the lives of large numbers of children and families through addressing national social issues, is one of the key rewards of the work. (Two examples of effective policy development relating adoption of special needs children and family preservation and support promoting permanency were previously shared in the nature of the work section.) Other rewards of the work include the challenges and opportunities of interpreting complex legislation addressing nationally significant policy and practice and working with diverse stakeholders to implement programs.

The social worker as a policy analyst in federal child welfare who builds on skills from state agency experiences (e.g. supervision, contract management, or other program management, development or policy development/analysis) and the macro components of a Master of Social Work (MSW) program especially policy (foundation and specialized, e.g. child welfare policy), research, organizations, and administration finds rewards in the work. Likewise, similar components of the Doctor of Philosophy (Ph.D.) program and teaching in a social work program, e.g. child welfare policy, family preservation practice, and other related courses, not only provide rewards to the social worker as a policy analyst, but also to other developing social workers preparing for the work.

How to Get Started on This Career Track

In the current environment of increasing privatization efforts in federal programs, contract staff is now working side by side in the same federal programs with federal staff such as policy (program specialists) analysts in both the central offices in D.C. and regional offices. Social workers as program analysts are being hired as consultant reviewers and team leaders (e.g. Child and Family Services Reviews in the child welfare programs) through a consultant firm supported by the federal government.

There has been a limited number of state agency staff under the Intergovernmental Personnel Act (IPA) entering federal service for a limited amount of time and later becoming federal employees. Likewise, public or private sector staff in Master of Social Work programs has developed experience as policy analysts in their field placements in federal agencies and have later entered the federal workforce.

References

Adoption and Safe Families Act of 1997, Pub. L. No. 105-89, 111 Stat. 2115.

Adoption Assistance and Child Welfare Act of 1980, Pub. L. No. 96-272, 94 Stat. 500.

Bovbjerg, R. R. (1985). What is policy analysis? *Policy Analysis and Management, 1*(5), 154-158.

Dunn, W. N. (1981). *Public policy analysis: An introduction.* Englewood Cliffs, N.J.: Prentice-Hall, Inc.

Ginsberg, L. H. (2001). *Careers in social work* (2nd ed., Rev.). Needham Heights, MA: Allyn & Bacon.

Haynes, K. S., & Mickelson, J. S. (1997). *Affecting change: Social workers in the political arena* (3rd ed., Rev.). White Plains, N.Y.: Longman.

Majchrzak, A. (1984). *Methods for policy research.* Newbury Park, CA: Sage Publications, Inc.

Meltsner, A. J. (1976). *Policy analysts in the bureaucracy.* Berkley and Los Angeles, CA: University of California Press.

Newlin, P. (1997). Family preservation: Where have we been? How can we as social workers continue to collaborate? In J. Kelly-Lewis (Ed.),*Change and challenge: MCH social workers make a difference* (pp. 60-78). [U. S. Department of Health and Human Services, Public Health Service, Health Resources and Services Administration, Maternal and Child Health Bureau, Grant #MCJ009097]. Columbia, SC: College of Social Work.

Omnibus Budget Reconciliation Act of 1993, Pub. L. No 103-66.

16

ILLUMINATING THE ADDICTIVE
PROCESS AS A CLINICIAN

cd

Jane Abraham

Nature of the Work

Social Workers deal directly with clients on the emotional, spiritual, and physical bases of life. We learn to identify problems in these areas and help clients understand alternatives to their usual choices. Emotionally we may discover that a client is depressed and used chemicals to "fix" their depression. Spiritually we may ascertain that a client is full of guilt, shame, and remorse because of their need to maintain their addiction. Physically we may recognize that a client has allowed their body to become depleted of nutrients that are required to live a healthy life. Once we begin working with a client under the umbrella of the addictive process we notice that they may have lost interest in the major areas of life that most people find enjoyable. It is when we notice these areas that are out of balance that we find the challenge as clinicians. How can we best address the issues and assist clients in discovering their way through the maze of confusion that accompanies the addictive process?

First, let's take a look at "the addictive process." It is not easy to discern who is and who is not laboring with the disease of addiction, so maybe it is best to decide that addiction may be a process. Let's consider that a person who uses alcohol and other drugs as a way of altering feelings to change the way their life is perceived may not be the healthiest person from the start. After all, how healthy is it to address an issue with drugs? Does taking drugs really enhance life or is it just a social lubricant that helps people feel less inhibited? How healthy is it to ingest chemicals to alter the brain chemistry? What's the point? What does the need to do that say about the person who is involved in the process? Is there an underlying need to mask the discomfort the person may feel in a setting? What is the possibility of addressing the primary issue of social anxiety directly rather than taking a drug to alter the uncomfortable feeling? So if we look at the process we may notice that anyone who uses chemicals to alter their feelings may just as well learn to change their attitude and adjust their perceptions of self in relation to others. Using chemicals, even a glass of wine, is a placebo effect if we look at the issue directly. Then there are those who are unable to drink a single glass of wine, but two bottles into the evening are unable to function safely or productively. However, to ask them you might find they are "just fine" in their own minds only tomorrow to realize they had no awareness of the evening and how it unfolded because they were in blackout after the first half of the first bottle.

We want to look directly at this because this is what it takes to recognize a problem arising in the addictive process. When screening an individual for therapy we must learn to ask the questions that steer us into discovering the client's pattern of use of alcohol and other drugs. Often as clinicians we don't even think that is something pertinent to why a person may have come to us asking for assistance. Nonetheless, we may soon discover that the client in question has all of these negative consequences in their lives because of their choice to continue to use alcohol and other drugs after they have crossed into the addictive process.

It is for us to determine the diagnoses of our clients and if we do not ask the correct questions we may not get the correct answers. Clients with addictive disorders very often minimize their use of chemicals because they do not want anyone to think they are "weak." It is our job as professionals to uncover their fear and illuminate their choices so they may make a determination about how they want to continue living their lives. We, first of all, must understand that addiction is not a sign of weakness. It is earmarked with all the signs of a disease as determined by the American Medical Association in 1955. Therefore, we as clinicians must begin to shift our perceptions from a moral issue to an idea that the client is unable to control their choices once they have moved into the disease of addiction. That is a mighty thin line we are talking about so we must have thorough training to be able to diagnose addictive processes. If we take a look at the brain chemistry we will notice quickly that the chemistry of a person with an addictive disorder reacts differently than others who do not have the disease. We may be unable to do the actual lab work, but we can discern the difference in a clinical setting by listening to the client talk about what has been happening in their lives for a period of time. We may soon discover that if they were able to stop using chemicals they would have, but they reached a point where they were truly unable to stop using regardless of the consequences.

Training and Degrees Required

Social work is the most well thought out profession that I know. As social workers we are trained to identify the problems and issues that our clients face on every level. Not only do we recognize the social barriers, we are trained to know what to do about them. We have an expansive knowledge base that allows us to diagnose and address myriad issues faced by our clients and their families. Today we have a national social work credential that allows us to specialize in the treatment of those in the addictive process.

The Certified-Clinical Alcohol, Tobacco, and Other Drug Social Worker (C-CATODSW) credential was developed to give credibility to those of us who work in the addictions field. First, you must have a Master's degree in social work. The training that is required to be determined competent for that credential is thorough. It involves knowing the functions as a clinician who works with others to understand their addictive process. Screening is one area that is stressed. It is through screening by asking the right questions that we may learn what is really happening to our clients. There are several primary areas of focus such as screening, reports and records, etiology, education, counseling, referral, and continuum of care that an addiction professional will learn about and continue their education. One of the most serious areas we learn to honor is confidentiality and anonymity of our clients. There is federal legislation in this area to protect the client's rights. There are particular techniques we learn to identify clients and their issues without divulging their identity and lessening their chances to remain anonymous. The C-CATODSW credential requires continuing education specific to the field of addictions.

Counseling those involved in the addictive process is often more demanding than some other areas. As clinicians we have a need to understand the disease of addiction and how it breaks down in the chemistry of the brain. We have a need to understand the problems that arise in the family structure as a direct result of the addictive process. We need to be able to show our clients the breakdown of their employment when they have lost a job or find it is in jeopardy because of their addictive process. We must be able to help them walk through any legal ramifications that may arise due to their use of chemicals. We may want to help them understand their loss of spiritual contact because of the feelings of shame and remorse. We will want to help them adjust to losing their best coping mechanism. All these areas are essential aspects of the addictive process and the recovery process. We will need to help them understand that the people they used to spend time with may not be helpful to them in their recovery process because those same people may be the ones with whom our client actively used chemicals.

It is no small matter when assisting someone to evaluate his or her life through the eyes of recovery. They may not fully understand the intricacies involved when we inform them that they will need to change people, places, and things to be successful in their bid for recovery. That involves taking a long, hard look at their families, which more often than not will require changes in how they relate in that area as well. So, we reach a point where clients have to make some of the hardest choices of their lives in order to find solid recovery as a way of life. We can and do recommend that they become involved in self-help groups by going to meetings and getting a sponsor to help them learn to live life without the use of chemicals. Most importantly, we help them realize that therapy is an important factor in their recovery because they may not be able to address the deeper issues that arise in recovery through self-help meetings and sponsorship.

As clinicians we spend a lot of time, energy, and money learning the newest developments for treating our clients. We may learn EMDR, Acupuncture Detoxification, Hypnosis, Psychospiritual Integrative Breathwork and other interventions that are not necessarily practiced on a daily basis, but nonetheless, prove to be the saving grace for our clients. In the nearly 20 years I have been in the field of addictions I have learned these techniques and more only to observe over and over again as they help clients move into wellness. With that said, let me take a line or two to encourage you as a professional to continue your education in order to present the "cutting edge" interventions to your clients.

Continue to do your personal work through exploring the incredible tools that find themselves in your reality. Do not stop. Discover the joy of learning as much as you can to help heal the ailing client emotionally, spiritually, and physically. Then you can share with your clients and watch their miraculous healing by using tools whose value you know because you have explored them on a personal basis.

The process of addiction is not an easy issue to address, but the successful choices of a client by far can make it the most rewarding. I invite you to begin your education toward the specialty of addictions and hope that you find your journey exciting. If you discover that it makes your soul sing then you have touched upon that which keeps me focused and enjoying the opportunities that arise when working in the field of addictions.

Types of Groups

As a clinician you will have an opportunity to work with individuals, couples, and families. If you work in an agency setting you will probably discover that you will provide client education in a group setting. You may address such diverse issues as the disease of addiction, family roles, or self-esteem. You will provide individual therapy to assist clients in their deeper issues that may not best be suited for group process. When families or employers are involved you may discover that you are a mediator advocating for your client. You will find yourself in various situations with the staff that places you in the position of advocating for your client. All in all the many hats of a social worker in the addiction field is varied and full of opportunities to explore and expand your knowledge base.

If you are working in private practice you may discover that you have a unique opportunity to assist your client on an individual basis toward a fulfilling and rewarding life without chemical interventions. You may also discover the need to consult with other professionals regarding medication for those who exhibit co-occurring disorders. Then you may discover that you are an observer to your client's progress and communicate with your consult to make certain your client's needs are being met with medication adjustments as needed.

Personality Traits and Skills Deemed
Important to Succeed

When I started working in the field of addictions it was common for any individual to be approved for a minimum of 28 days of residential treatment. That time element seemed too little to address the issues of learning to live life without the use of chemicals. Today, these unfortunate clients commonly are allotted only two residential days and are more than blessed to be granted eight days. Times have changed due to managed care and the utilization review process set up by insurance companies, thus drastically changing the clinician's method of treatment. Today, recovery is a difficult process with relapse built into the experience when relapse once was unacceptable.

Clients with the emotional, spiritual, and physical issues that come with chemical dependency face major changes in the way they live their lives. If you can imagine a place where everything with which you have been familiar no longer brings the balance of the moment, but rather brings devastation. What once was a pleasureful result in massive breakdowns in the major areas of life such as emotional, family, legal, physical, spiritual, and recreational. What used to result in "having a good time" often results in not remembering what happened when under the influence while in a state of blackout, which is when the client used to the point of not remembering the event.

Clinicians must reach a point of empathy that allows them to find a solid foundation for helping clients cope with issues that arise when the line of addiction is crossed into the area where devastation is the consequence of a choice to use chemicals. Often crossing the line of addiction brings with it a lifestyle that the client might otherwise not live. The clinician will be placed in a position of remaining single-minded in the pursuit of freedom from addiction to move beyond the unhealthy choices into a more balanced way of life without judgment or counter transference. It is a challenge to allow clients to make unhealthy choices that lead them back to their old habits of coping with life by using chemicals to ease the pain of the moment when the pain of the moment may be as mundane as the fact that it rained when the client planned a picnic. It doesn't take much for a client to throw away with both hands what was eagerly sought after in their journey toward recovery.

The joy of being a professional working with the addictive process exhibits when a client "gets it" and doesn't relapse, but keeps their foot to the path with willingness to pursue a new way of life. It is worth the frustration that accompanies clients making choices to continue living the way they always have to see the change in someone emotionally, spiritually, and physically when they make the decision and take the necessary actions to change their choices and ultimately the consequences. As a clinician we have the opportunity to present clients with various techniques that can and will help them in their trial and error process of recovery. It is a long an arduous path that often stops with the insurance companies long before the client is capable of implementing the necessary changes in their lives. Therefore, as a social worker, the sliding scale becomes a fact of life. It becomes essential to provide a therapeutic environment that does not add to the already incredible pressure of total abstinence.

Many clinicians do not understand the concept of total abstinence so I want to address the issue of chemical dependency. If you make a decision to work in the field of addictions you must be able to make the distinction between substance abuse and the disease of addiction. Quite simply an abuser is one who can set aside any chemical, be it alcohol, cocaine, marijuana, heroin, amphetamines, Benzodiazapines, or ecstasy with impunity never to pick it up again or even think about it seriously. A person with the disease of addiction is one who cannot set anything aside, but rather moves from one substance to another trying to find one that works for them, in that they can control it without experiencing negative consequences. That is not something easily understood so I shall simply state that the individual with the disease of addiction experiences emotional, spiritual, and physical problems as a direct result of the use of any chemical—even medications prescribed by their physicians. They cannot use chemicals successfully because their brain chemistry cannot discern the difference between a prescription and a street drug or alcohol.

Often it takes a while to get to that reality with a client in a therapeutic setting on an outpatient basis because working with someone in an outpatient setting allows them the freedom to continue their daily routine while addressing concerns that very often leave them in a state of vulnerability. This state of vulnerability may carry them into chemical usage as a means of coping with the pain that arises from a therapeutic intervention. As clinicians, we are afforded the opportunity to observe and illuminate that coping mechanism if we know how to ask the correct questions.

Difficulties of the Work

So what it gets to quickly, is asking the correct questions of our clients. This is part of the screening process that is on going during our therapeutic intervention. If we stay alert to what our client's tell us we automatically see a red flag when they begin to mention chemical usage as a means of coping with the issues that arise in their lives. The screening process then becomes a tool that helps us identify the underlying cause of many problems that arise in the life of a person who is in the addictive process. So let us look at some questions that we might use to uncover some of the denial that comes with the addictive process.

First, it might behoove you to notice any signs of the addictive process that may be overtly displayed by a client. For instance, is your client obese or extremely thin, do they have dilated pupils, visible tremors, difficulty sitting still, or a tendency to fall asleep during the session? These are some visible signs that are easily recognized by a clinician. If you see signs of this nature take time to ask direct questions. Being direct is often difficult to do with diplomacy, so practice before you begin asking questions of your clients. Screening for the correct diagnosis is essential and the questions you ask as a clinician are the way you will discover the accurate diagnosis. Even if there are no overt signs of an addictive process, asking the correct questions may assist your client in recognizing other ways of coping that exclude the use of chemicals.

Here is a list of 20 questions that you may want to ask your client:

1. Do you use alcohol, tobacco, caffeine, or other drugs?
2. What chemicals do you use?
3. How often do you use these chemicals?
4. How much do you use when you use?
5. Have you ever received a citation for driving under the influence (DUI)?
6. Have you ever been arrested for possession of an illegal substance?
7. Do you have any physical problems that require medication?
8. Do you have any emotional problems that require medication?
9. Do you take any prescribed medications?
10. What do you take?
11. Does a physician or psychiatrist prescribe it?
12. Do you take it as prescribed?
13. Has anyone expressed concern that you use chemicals too much?
14. Have you ever thought you use chemicals too much?
15. Have you lost jobs, relationships, or money due to the addictive process?
16. Have you ever tried to stop using all chemicals?
17. How long is the longest you have ever gone without using any chemicals?
18. Why did the total abstinence end?
19. Have you ever been treated for addictive disorders?
20. Do you want to address chemical usage during our time together?

These are fairly simplistic questions that may stir the proverbial pot before you finish asking them. Be prepared for that to happen when you begin probing into someone's usage of chemicals. This is an area which someone involved in the addictive process will protect by any means necessary in order to continue using to "fix their feelings." They may even stop coming to therapy in order to avoid the real issues at hand. Don't be surprised or hurt. Denial is part of the addictive process. Continue to assist your client in their work and ask the Universe to guide them to their next step in their process, which may or may not be you.

Rewards of the Work

All in all I'd say that working with others during the addictive process is a most rewarding profession. It is through the difficult times of a client awakening to the issues at hand that the clinician gets an opportunity to watch the unfolding of someone's life to healthiness. Being tolerant of clients during the discovery process is as important as being patient with them through the realization of their recovery process. The two are vastly different and cannot be mistaken one for the other.

In the discovery process we understand very quickly that the client is interested in learning about what has been happening to them resulting in such devastating consequences. It is during this early phase that we see the glimmer that starts in their eyes to become the flame of knowing in the future. Helping a client to realize the problems of their life stem from their choice to use chemicals is often time consuming and wrought with backsliding into the use of chemicals. I stated earlier that relapse has become part of the recovery process. It has never been part of the addictive process because use during addiction is not relapse, but use of chemicals without needing to label it as relapse. However, in recovery today there is an accepted relapse piece that comes with therapeutic endeavors to reach a client in denial. It may be accepted, but it is not encouraged. Help your clients understand the need for total abstinence.

Relapse is just another excuse that allows a client to use with a sense of impunity. In other words, no consequences if they use a little bit here and there. The problem with that is someone who has crossed the line of addiction cannot use just a little bit here and there. They go overboard very quickly. For instance, if someone has been working with you for six months and has not used any chemicals for four months they may think they can use successfully so they smoke marijuana or crack cocaine or drink a beer. The first time they do that they may be able to walk away from the event without getting too stoned, sprung, or drunk. They may think they have the addiction beat so the next time they may think they can use more or they may need to use more to get the same feeling they got before by using less. Whatever the event, the fact is that they will inevitably use more if they continue to use at all. That is the nature of the disease. It takes more of a substance to reach the desired effect. So, before they realize what has happened they are back to using more than they ever did and beginning to experience the severity of the negative consequences even more rapidly than they did before they started the therapeutic process with you. This is the proverbial snake eating its own tail. It is very circular and seems to happen with every single person in the addictive process.

The beauty of therapeutic intervention is the "high" is no longer as satisfying as it was before awakening to the disease. When a client is educated to the fact that they are the ones making the choice to continue their life down the "lose-lose" path, they tend to make note of their choice in the moment. That doesn't often deter them from stepping back on that path, but it does help them become aware that they are the ones making the choice again and again. It is at that point that they may truly awaken to the facts of life as an addict and decide to go down another path.

This reminds me of a story I heard when I first got into the field of addictions. A person was walking down a road and fell into a hole. He struggled diligently and finally found his way out of the hole. The next day he was walking down the same road and fell into the same hole. He had more difficulty getting out this time because he had lost some footing that he destroyed the day before. But eventually he got out of the hole and noticed that was a really difficult process. The next day he walked down that same road and fell into that same hole and struggled unbelievably to get out. He had to dig new footholds and handholds, but managed to get out. He was exhausted emotionally spiritually and physically. The next day he looked down that same road and decided to take another road. We, as clinicians, are the new footholds and handholds that the person can grab onto to get out of the old patterns. We give them the ability to identify the need to travel down a new road.

Some of the new footholds and handholds have to do with how thoroughly we are trained as clinical social workers. We are given the opportunity to learn and grow in the field of addictions while watching the transformation of our clients. Recovery is not a matter of simply setting aside the addiction. It is a matter of learning to live life on life's terms without the addictive process as a means of coping. No easy matter for the client of the clinician.

How to Get Started on This Career Track

To get started a social worker will need to get a job in the field of addictions whether it is chemical dependency, eating disorders, or gambling, to name only a few. There are many ways to get the hands-on experience required to receive a credential that calls you an addiction specialist. Attend continuing education events that focus on the addictive process. Get a supervisor who can teach you how to work with clients who are involved in the addictive process. Attend Twelve Core Function workshops to learn how to

LIST OF CONTRIBUTORS

Reverend Jane Abraham, LCSW, C-CATODSW LADAC, NCAC II, CADC II, ICADC, ADS, SAP is the president of The Healing Arts Research and Training Center in Memphis, Tennessee.

Rosemary Bell, MSW is a group therapist at Women's Haven Counseling Center in Fort worth, Texas.

Monica A. Carbajal, MSW, LMSW is a social worker working for AIDS Outreach of Tarrant County in Fort Worth, Texas.

Kim Denton is a director of North Central Indiana Rural Crisis Center, INC in Rensselaer, Indiana.

Cynthia A. Faulkner, PhD is an assistant professor at Morehead State University in Morehead, Kentucky.

Samuel S. Faulkner, PhD is an assistant professor at Morehead State University in Morehead, Kentucky.

Santos Hernandez, PhD is dean of the school of social work at University of Texas at Arlington in Arlington, Texas.

Pamela Jenkins, MSW is a medical social worker at Cincinnati Children's Hospital in Cincinnati, Ohio.

Seth Knobel, BSW is a school social worker at Skokie High School in Skokie, Illinois.

Adam R. Malson, MS, NCC is the director of career services at Saint Joseph's College in Rensselaer, Indiana.

Irvin Moore, Jr., MSW, MDiv is a hospital chaplain at Cincinnati Children's Hospital in Cincinnati, Ohio.

Patricia Newlin, Ph.D., LMSW-AP is a social policy analyst at the U.S. Department of Health and Human Services Administration for Children and Families in Dallas, Texas.

Tuyen D. Nguyen, PhD is an assistant professor at California State University—Fullerton in Fullerton, California.

Derek Robertson, M.Ed., LPC, is a licensed counselor working for AIDS Outreach of Tarrant County in Fort Worth, Texas.

Shawna Stewart, MA, LPC is a licensed counselor working for AIDS Outreach of Tarrant County in Fort Worth, Texas.

Cathy Ticen, MA, LMHC is a licensed therapist and clinic director at Wabash Valley Hospital in Rensselaer, Indiana.

Tina Vickery, BSW is a social worker at Rensselaer Healthcare Center in Rensselaer, Indiana.

David Weed, MA, LMHC is a licensed mental health counselor at Saint Joseph's College in Rensselaer, Indiana.